Pioneers of modern typography

Revised edition

Pioneers

of modern typography

Herbert Spencer

The MIT Press   Cambridge, Massachusetts

First MIT Press paperback edition, 1983
First edition 1969
Revised edition 1982
Second printing 1985
©1969, 1982 Herbert Spencer
Published by
Lund Humphries Publishers Ltd
Printed and bound in Great Britain

Library of Congress Cataloging in
Publication Data
Spencer, Herbert, 1924–
    Pioneers of modern typography.
    Originally published 1969,
    2nd rev. ed. London:
Lund Humphries, 1982
    Bibliography: p.
    1. Printing – History.
    2. Art, Modern – 20th century – History.
    I. Title.
    Z116.A3S6 1983 686.2'09 82–12695
ISBN 0–262–69081–0 (pbk.)

Since the publication of the first edition of this book in 1969 interest in the work of artists and designers of the inter-war period has grown enormously. During recent years there have been several exhibitions and a number of well-researched publications which have greatly added to our knowledge of the period.

In preparing this new edition I have received the generous help and advice of many friends· Edith Tschichold, Herbert Bayer, and Nely Zwart have provided additional material to illustrate this volume. I have been greatly assisted in the task of selecting and obtaining the illustrations for this edition by my daughter, Mafalda Spencer, whose research into Dutch typographic design of the 1920s and 1930s has brought to light several significant new examples. She also contributed the essay on Werkman included in this volume.

Herbert Spencer

Contents

Top row (left to right): Theo van
Doesburg, H.N.Werkman, Alexander
Rodchenko.
Centre row: Herbert Bayer, Jan
Tschichold, Paul Schuitema.
Right: El Lissitzky.

Left: L. Moholy-Nagy
Piet Zwart (on the left) with H. P. Berlage.

Above: Kurt Schwitters
Right: The meeting of Constructivists and Dadaists in Weimar, 1922. Theo van Doesburg (in paper hat) with El Lissitzky (smoking pipe) behind him, and Tristan Tzara (with walking stick), Hans Arp (extreme right), and Hans Richter (lying on the ground).

One cannot carry everywhere the corpse of one's father.

Guillaume Apollinaire

The new man should have the courage to be new.

Raoul Hausmann, 1921

You may paint with whatever material you please, with pipes, postage stamps, postcards or playing cards, candelabra, pieces of oil cloth, collars, painted paper, newspapers.

Guillaume Apollinaire, 1913

The word and the image are one.

Hugo Ball, 1917

Not world visions, B U T – world reality.

El Lissitsky

Our art had to be young, it had to be new, it had to integrate all the experimental tendencies of the futurists and the cubists. Above all, our art had to be international, for we believed in an Internationale of the spirit . . .

Richard Huelsenbeck, 1916

All doors and windows must be opened wide, so that the musty smell we have had to breathe since childhood can disappear.

Bruno Jasienski, 1921

It is Marinetti who instilled in me the feeling of the ocean and the power of the machine.

Benito Mussolini

Contrast is the mark of our age.

Theo van Doesburg, 1926

Catalogues, posters, advertisements of all sorts. Believe me, they contain the poetry of our epoch.

Guillaume Apollinaire

Paint with photos, write poetry with photos!

John Heartfield

The new book demands new writers.

El Lissitzky

The new typography is not a fashion.

Jan Tschichold

In Weimar, I have radically turned everything upside down. This is the famous Academy with the most modern teachers! Every evening I have spoken to the students and have scattered the poison of the new spirit. De Stijl will soon reappear in a more radical form. I have mountains of strength and I now know that our ideas will triumph over everything and everybody.

Theo van Doesburg, 1921

Contrast is perhaps the most important element in all modern design.

Jan Tschichold

Typography must be clear communication in its most vivid form ... clarity is the essence of modern printing.

L. Moholy-Nagy, 1923

For modern advertising and for the modern exponent of form the individual element – the artist's 'own touch' – is of absolutely no consequence.

El Lissitzky

The knowledge of photography is just as important as that of the alphabet. The illiterate of the future will be the person ignorant of the camera as well as of the pen.

L. Moholy-Nagy

Art must break with the practices of the perfumed, peverse, hypersensitive, hysterical, romantic, individualistic, boudoir-type art of yesterday. It must create a new language of forms, available to all and in harmony with the rhythm of life.

Henryk Berlewi, 1924

Criminals in Russia were formerly branded on the back with a red diamond ◇ and deported to Siberia ... here in Weimar the Bauhaus puts its stamp – the red square – on everything front and back.

El Lissitzky, 1923

Sanserif is the type of the present day.

Jan Tschichold

Colour is a creative element, not a trimming.

Piet Zwart

Concepts should be expressed with the greatest economy.

El Lissitzky

A photograph neither lies nor tells the truth.

John Heartfield

In centred typography, pure form comes before the meaning of the words.

Jan Tschichold

The more uninteresting a letter, the more useful it is to the typographer.

Piet Zwart

H. N. Werkmann, 1924.
From *the next call*
4. published on the
occasion of Lenin's
death

The roots of modern typography are entwined with those of twentieth-century painting, poetry, and architecture. Photography, technical changes in printing, new reproduction techniques, social changes, and new attitudes have also helped to erase the frontiers between the graphic arts, poetry, and typography and have encouraged typography to become more visual, less linguistic, and less purely linear.

The new vocabulary of typography and graphic design was forged during a period of less than twenty years. The 'heroic' period of modern typography may be said to have begun with Marinetti's *Figaro* manifesto in 1909 and to have reached its peak during the early 'twenties. By the end of that decade it had entered a new and different phase, one of consolidation rather than of exploration and innovation.

But of course modern typography was not the abrupt invention of one man or even of one group. It emerged in response to new demands and new opportunities thrown up by the nineteenth century. The violence with which modern typography burst upon the early twentieth-century scene reflected the violence with which new concepts in art and design in every field were sweeping away exhausted conventions and challenging those attitudes which had no relevance to a highly industrialized society.

The revolution in typography paid scant regard to the traditions of the printing industry. But we must remember that it took place at a period when the industry had largely lost sight of those traditions and that the revolution was carried through by painters, writers, poets, architects, and others who came to printing from outside the industry. These men were bursting with ideas and exhilerated by a new concept of art and society who were determined to make their voices heard effectively. They seized upon printing with fervour because they clearly recognized it for what it properly is – a potent means of conveying ideas and information – and not for what much of it had then become – a kind of decorative art remote from the realities of contemporary society.

During the nineteenth century the printing industry had failed properly to recognize the fundamental changes which were taking place in society and consequently in the nature of what was printed. The rapid growth of industrialization and of mass-production had created demands for new kinds of printing, first to control efficiently the processes of production and distribution and later, as production and competition increased, to create and to stimulate demand through advertising. During the

BLAST First (from politeness) **ENGLAND**

CURSE ITS CLIMATE FOR ITS SINS AND INFECTIONS

DISMAL SYMBOL, SET round our bodies,
of effeminate lout within.

VICTORIAN VAMPIRE, the LONDON cloud sucks
the TOWN'S heart.

A 1000 MILE LONG, 2 KILOMETER Deep

BODY OF WATER even, is pushed against us

from the Floridas, TO MAKE US MILD.

OFFICIOUS MOUNTAINS keep back DRASTIC WINDS

SO MUCH VAST MACHINERY TO PRODUCE

THE CURATE of "Eltham"
BRITANNIC ÆSTHETE
WILD NATURE CRANK
DOMESTICATED
                  POLICEMAN
LONDON COLISEUM
SOCIALIST-PLAYWRIGHT
DALY'S MUSICAL COMEDY
GAIETY CHORUS GIRL
TONKS

We lived beneath the mat,
Warm and snug and fat,
But one woe, and that
Was the Cat!

To our joys
a clog, In
our eyes a
fog, On our
hearts a log,
Was the Dog!

When the
Cat's away,
Then
The mice
will
play,
But alas!
one day, (So they say)

Came the Dog and
Cat, hunting
for a
Rat,
Crushed
the mice
all flat,
Each
one
as
he
sat,
Underneath
the mat, Warm and snug and fat,
Think of
that!

Three examples of visual poetry: by
Christian Morgenstern, 1905, Man Ray,
1924, and a typewriter composition by
Pietro Saga, 1926.

A 'tiksel' produced by H.N. Werkman during the 1920s.

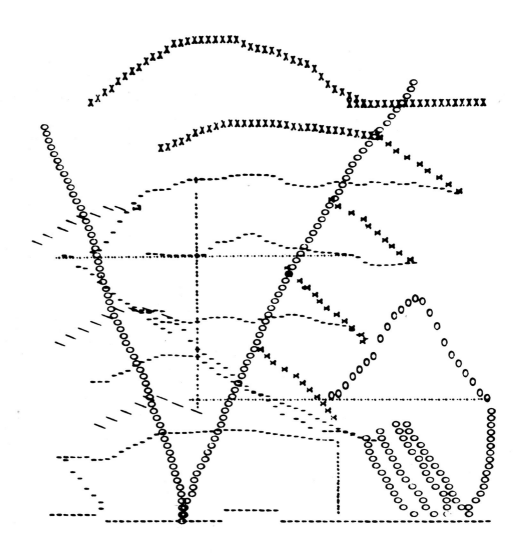

nineteenth century, as the superlatives increased, printing types had grown bigger, fatter, and more exuberant, but the printer still clung to a layout based on that of the book. The first real departure from the centred layout of the book printer was introduced by the exponents of 'Artistic Printing' during the 1870's, but the significance and potentialities of this development were obscured by the elaborate ornament and decoration – often quite unrelated to the subject matter of the text – in which they shrouded their printed announcements. The Artistic Printing movement contained the seed of modern typography, but the seed fell upon infertile ground. By the end of the century most printers were imprisoned in a web of sterile convention or involved in an orgy of technical gimmickry, and the design of most of what they produced was either boring or irrelevant. It was as a reaction to this situation that the Futurists adopted their aggressive new technique for putting their notions into print.

The first Cubist compositions painted by Braque and Picasso in 1908 were but tentative steps towards a new horizon. Of greater immediate significance to the development of modern typography was Marinetti's *Manifesto of Futurism*, published in the French newspaper, *Le Figaro*, on 20 February 1909. This defined, in strident tones, a new concept of art and design. Twelve months later, in Milan, the *Manifesto of Futurist Painting* was signed by five painters, including Balla and Boccioni. Boccioni, who was also a sculptor, became one of the principal theorists of Futurism. His manifesto on Futurist sculpture published in 1912 anticipated the mobile constructions later projected by Gabo, in 1922, and those made by Calder, in 1930.

Futurism was a violent reaction against the *status quo* and the oppressive weight of the past. It enthusiastically embraced modern civilization and recognized the beauty of machines. The Futurists sought new forms that would enable them to break the limitations of two dimensions and to express 'revolution and movement' without resorting to illusionary visual effects. The violent, incendiary technique of propaganda which they used was later widely imitated throught Europe – by the Dadaists in France and Switzerland and Germany, by the Constructivists in Russia, and by de Stijl in Holland, among others.

The Futurists were opposed to art for art's sake and they equally rejected any notion of merely playing with form or of indulging in typographic innovation for its own sake. In typography, they demanded that the form should intensify the content. In 1909 Marinetti wrote: 'The book will be the futurist expression of our futurist

Cœur couronne et miroir

MON CŒUR PAREIL À UNE FLAMME RENVERSÉE

LES ROIS QUI MEURENT
TOUR A TOUR
RENAISSENT AU CŒUR DES POÈTES

DANS CE MIROIR JE SUIS ENCLOS VIVANT ET VRAI COMME ON IMAGINE LES ANGES ET NON COMME SONT LES REFLETS

Guillaume Apollinaire

La cravate et la montre

LA CRAVATE
DOU
LOU
REUSE
QUE TU
PORTES
ET QUI T'
ORNE O CI
VILISÉ
OTE-   TU VEUX
LA   BIEN
SI   RESPI
       RER

COMME L'ON S'AMUSE BIEN

les heures

et le
vers
dantesque
luisant et
cadavérique

le bel
inconnu

Il
est
—
5
en
fin

Et
tout
se
ra
fi
ni

les Muses
aux portes de
ton corps

l'infini
redressé
par un fou
de philosophe

la
beau
Mon
cœur   té
de
la
les
yeux   vie
pas
se
l'enfant la
dou
leur
Agla   de
mou
rir

semaine   la main

Tircis

Two 'lyrical ideograms' by Guillaume Apollinaire, 1914, in each of which the typography is used to stress the essence of the poem. Apollinaire also called such works 'figurative poems', 'ideogrammatic poems', and, finally, 'calligrammes'.

consciousness. I am against what is known as the harmony of a setting. When necessary, we shall use three or four columns to a page and twenty different type faces. We shall represent *hasty perceptions* in *italic* and express a **scream** in **bold** type . . . a new, painterly, typographic representation will be born on the printed page.'

The influence of Futurism spread rapidly eastwards. Marinetti's *Figaro* manifesto had been immediately relayed to Russia and there are reports that Marinetti himself visited St Petersburg in 1910. However, we know for certain only that he lectured in Moscow and St Petersburg early in 1914, by which time the Futurist movement was firmly established there. Larionov, Goncharova, and Malevich were the principal Russian Futurist painters.

In Moscow, Larionov's Rayonist compositions and, in Munich, the works of the Russian Wassily Kandinsky were the most purely abstract paintings of 1911 and 1912, but in 1913 Kasimir Malevich took the final, inevitable stride towards pure abstraction when he exhibited a pencil drawing, *Quadrat*, which was, to quote his own description, 'nothing more or less than a black square upon a white ground'. This first Suprematist picture was followed by a second, *Circle*, and then by another pencil drawing consisting of two squares and a series of simple geometric compositions. Malevich described Suprematism as 'the supremacy of pure feeling or perception in the pictorial arts', and of his first Suprematist picture he wrote: 'it was no "empty square" which I had exhibited, but rather the experience of non-objectivity'.

Suprematism provided the basis for much geometrical abstract painting in Europe during the next two decades, and through the work of Lissitzky, Rodchenko, and Moholy-Nagy during the early 'twenties Malevich's ideas and those of the Constructivist Vladimir Tatlin had immense influence on the development of modern typography and graphic design.

The Futurists regarded violence as good in itself and believed war to have value as 'a hygienic purge'. But in contrast to this, in Zurich, in 1916, a new movement, Dadaism, was born out of disillusionment with war, and disgust at the slaughter of millions on the battlefields of Europe. The pioneers of this movement were Hans Arp, Hugo Ball, and Tristan Tzara. The Dadaists, in revolt against the obsolescence, the stupidity, and the rot which had led to the first world war, upheld the supremacy of man and the value of art. They sought, in the words of Arp, 'to establish a balance between heaven

Apollinaire took little direct interest in how his calligrammes were translated into type. This is his manuscript for *Il Pleut*, written in red and black ink on a page torn from an exercise book, and, opposite, as it was set by M. Levé, the printer of the review *S I C* (*Sons Ideés Couleurs*), in which it first appeared in 1916.

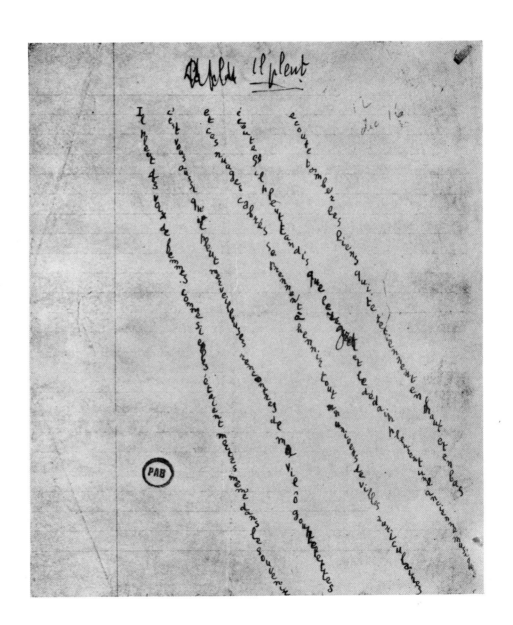

IL PLEUT

Il pleut des voix de femmes comme si elles étaient mortes même dans le souvenir

c'est vous aussi qu'il pleut merveilleuses rencontres de ma vie ô gouttelettes

et ces nuages cabrés se prennent à hennir tout un univers de villes auriculaires

écoute s'il pleut tandis que le regret et le dédain pleurent une ancienne musique

écoute tomber les liens qui te retiennent en haut et en bas

GUILLAUME APOLLINAIRE

Poesia vertice raggiante dell'universo
Anche i tuoi vestiti mortali sono adorabili

Antiche cose con polpa e nervo
Esseri vivi col loro destino terrestre
Ombre ora confitte in un segno netto e fermo
Tipi transustanziazione di misteri infiniti

Alfabeti lettere dentelles batiste fiocchi
Ornamenti dell'idea nuda
Je m'abìme dans ce fouilli de tiédeurs charnelles
Respiro i ricchi odori delle tue segretezze
Bacio le ciarpe d'oro che sono un poco del tuo grande corpo

Vecchio satiro cosmopolita di mitologie future
Voilà ti posseggo tutta

A powerful example of Futurist typography from *Bif§zf + 18 Simultaneità Chimismi lirici* by Ardengo Soffici, Florence, 1915.

and hell'. The Dadaists parodied the values of a bankrupt society and used the weapons of ridicule and shock to demonstrate the absurdity of established values. In making their ironical comments on the follies of this world, the Dadaists utilized the Cubist technique of collage, but Kurt Schwitters, especially, in his MERZ pictures composed of rubbish, delved deeper into the wastepaper basket than the Cubists had done.

Schwitter's MERZ pictures, the first of which he produced in 1919, and the works of Höch and Hausmann, fantasies in which reality was juxtaposed with the absurd, indicated the potentialities of photomontage – a technique that was later to be used with great impact in political propaganda by Rodchenko, in Russia, and by Heartfield, in Germany, and in advertising by Schuitema and by Zwart, in Holland. Surrealism, a schismatic offshoot of Dadaism which emerged in Paris in 1924, also made extensive use of collage.

Alvin Langdon Coburn was one of the first photographers to recognize the significance of Cubism for photography, and in 1913 he exhibited in London a series of bird's-eye views of New York in which the distorted perspective reduced the streets and buildings to an abstract pattern. Four years later he set out to disprove the notion that the camera could not be 'abstract' and with the aid of three mirrors clamped together in a triangle he produced the series of non-objective photographs he called 'Vortographs'. The following year, 1918, a member of the Zurich Dada group, Christian Schad, produced a number of abstractions photographically but without the use of a camera. These 'Schadographs', which resemble the collages of the Cubists and of Kurt Schwitters, were created by placing flat objects and cut-out paper directly on to light-sensitive paper, but in 1921 the American Dadaist, Man Ray, considerably developed the technique by making use of three-dimensional objects and cast shadows in his 'Rayograms'. Moholy-Nagy, who was quick to recognize the significance of the new technique and to explore its possibilities, described it as 'the most completely dematerialized medium which the new vision commands'.

In 1917, a few months after the launching of Dadaism, de Stijl, one of the most influential groups of artists in this century, was founded by Theo van Doesburg at Leiden, in Holland. It included among its early members the painters Mondrian, Huszar, and van der Leck, the sculptor Vantongerloo, the writer Kok, and the architects Oud and Wils. Mondrian and van Doesburg were the group's principal

A page by the Italian Futurist leader, Filippo Tommaso Marinetti, from the first Dada publication, *Cabaret Voltaire*, edited by Hugo Ball, Zurich, 1916.

D U N E

7. 8.
Parole in libertà

VENTO

MOVIMENTO
DI
2 STANTUFFI

negatore pigrizia inerzia
congelare tutto con stelle
letterarie sradicate della carne
(NOTTE LIBRARIA)
seppellire tutto con odore di
ascelle materassi di profumi
mammelle cotte nel piacere
+ 7000 ragionamenti scettici

affermatore ottimismo
forza respingere il vento
pessimista caldo o freddo
andare senza scopo per
FARE VIVERE CORRERE
ESSERE

SANGUE

Karazuc zuczuc
Karazuc zuczuc
AAAAaaaaaaa
Nad I nad I

SOLE OLIATORE UNIVERSALE

MENU D'UN PRANZO DI 6 COPERTI
AL LUME DI UNA LUCCIOLA

tlac
tlac
cic-cioc

1. antipasto di kakawicknostalgin
2. angocette al sugo
3. rimorschif in bianco
4. presentimentlung allo spiedo
5. grappoli emorroidali
6. orina d'asceta frappée

aih
aiiiiii
aiiiiii
fuuuuut

sedersi com odamente in quattro
sulla punta d'uno spillo
suelleza signorile grigioperla del vento
che porta a spasso l'incendio-levrette-vestita-di-rosso

CIRCO EQUESTRE

(VIOLA INCERTO FANTASTICOMICO)

FOLLA CRETINERIA FOLLA FOLLA FOLLA

Difficile

Più difficile

Ancora più difficile

Difficilissimo

BASTA   BASTA   BASTA

silenzio

av volgere
si lenzio

OP

SIGNORA
INCINTA
TROPPA
EMOZIONE

(rapidissimo)

LA

paura

attesa

sospensione

BRAA......... VOOOoooooooooooOOOA

Luico Venna, Florence, 1917.

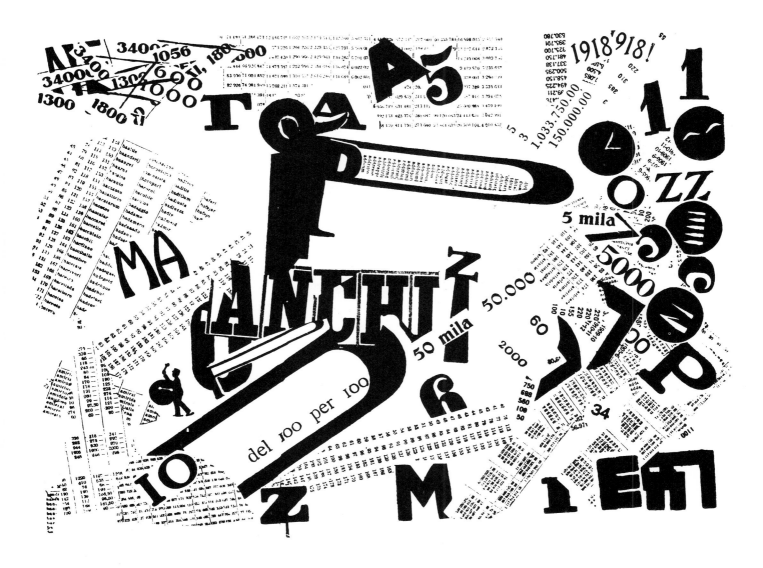

Direktion r. hausmann
Steglitz zimmermann
strasse 34

DER dada

50 Pfg.

dadadegie   hausmann - baader

3/ 3333/3333

5,0

$13 : 7 = 1,85714285\ldots$

60 40 50 10 30 20 60 40

Ach

3,14159

5.9.2 1 8.3.4.7.10 11.6

16,305

Jahr 1 des Weltfriedens. Avis dada

Hirsch Kupfer schwächer. Wird Deutschland verhungern? Dann muß es unterzeichnen. Fesche junge Dame, zweiundvierziger Figur für Hermann Loeb. Wenn Deutschland nicht unterzeichnet, so wird es wahrscheinlich unterzeichnen. Am Markt der Einheitswerte überwiegen die Kursrückgänge. Wenn aber Deutschland unterzeichnet, so ist es wahrscheinlich, daß es unterzeichnet um nicht zu unterzeichnen. Amorsäle. Achtuhrabendblattmitbrausendeshimmels. Von Viktorhahn. Loyd George meint, daß es möglich wäre, daß Clémenceau der Ansicht ist, daß Wilson glaubt, Deutschland müsse unterzeichnen, weil es nicht unterzeichnen nicht wird können. Infolgedessen erklärt der club dada sich für die absolute Preßfreiheit, da die Presse das Kulturinstrument ist, ohne das man nie erfahren würde, daß Deutschland endgültig nicht unterzeichnet, blos um zu unterzeichnen. (Club dada, Abt. für Preßfreiheit, soweit die guten Sitten es erlauben.)

Die neue Zeit beginnt mit dem Todesjahr des Oberdada

A d 1

Mitwirkende: Baader, Hausmann, Huelsenbeck, Tristan Tzara.

Cover of the first issue of the periodical
Der Dada, edited by Raoul Hausmann,
Berlin, 1919.

theorists, and they proclaimed that harmony in painting, architecture, and design
could be achieved only by adopting a style that was geometrically pure and
impersonal. The basis of de Stijl work was the rectangle and the use of black, white,
and grey, and the primary colours red, blue, and yellow. The work and ideas of the
members were widely disseminated through the group's journal, *de Stijl*, which first
appeared in August 1917 and continued to be published until 1932. During the early
'twenties, under the direction of van Doesburg, a man of exceptional versatility and an
active and voluble propagandist, the influence of de Stijl spread rapidly throughout
Europe.

Futurism, Dadaism, de Stijl, Suprematism and Constructivism were movements which
had originated in different countries and whose objectives were different and
sometimes conflicting, yet each in one way or another contributed significantly to the
shaping of modern typography and to the merging of word and image.

It was in Social Democratic Germany about 1921 that the main streams of the modern
movement converged. From East and from West all the new, raw ideas about art and
design poured in. In the aftermath of the first world war and of the Russian revolution,
Germany became the intellectual stock-pot of Europe.

Among the many young Russian intellectuals who arrived in Berlin at that time was
Lissitzky, who had studied engineering at Darmstadt before the war. Altman,
Archipenko, Ehrenburg, Gabo, Mayakovsky, Pasternak, and Antoine Pevsner were
also there. The Hungarian Moholy-Nagy had recently arrived from Vienna, and the
leader of de Stijl, van Doesburg, was a frequent visitor. Lissitzky was then 31. During
the previous two years, in Vitebsk, he had produced his first non-objective paintings,
which he called 'Prouns', and some designs for posters and book covers incorporating
drawn lettering, but in Berlin the more sophisticated printing facilities that were
available encouraged him to devote much of his time to typography. Between 1921
and 1924, when tuberculosis drove him into a sanatorium, his unflagging energy,
infectious enthusiasm, and enormous output of typographical designs, paintings, and
photographic experiments made him one of the principal channels through which the
ideas of the Constructivists and Suprematists permeated Western Europe. He travelled
untiringly and was in touch with all the leading personalities of the modern movement
in Germany, Switzerland, Holland, France and Poland. With Ilya Ehrenburg, in Berlin
he edited the Constructivist magazine *Veshch*; he collaborated with Kurt Schwitters

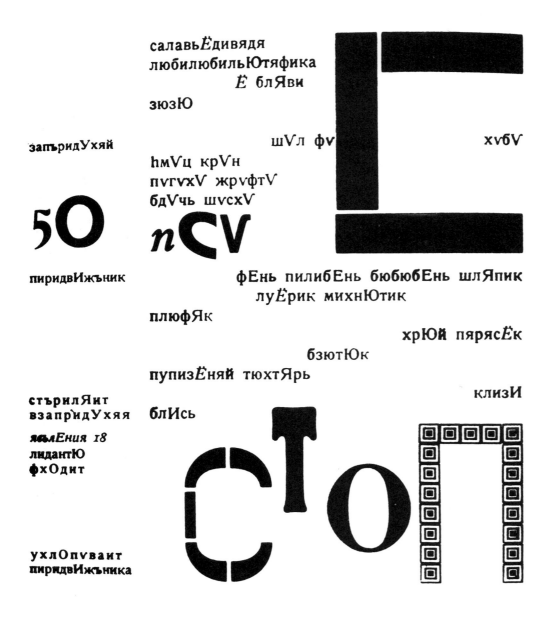

THé â t r e 👉 MICHEL
40 rUe Des mathurINS

venDredI 6 et saMedI 7
juiLLet 1923

SOirée
du CœEUR à BARBE

la grande semaine
a été prolongée
jusqu'au 7 juillet

👈

OcatiOn :

OrganISée paR TCHéREZ !

Prix
Une place de loge .... 30 fr.
Fauteuil d'orchestre..... 25 fr.
Fauteuil de balcon
        1ᵉʳ rang..... 15 fr.
Fauteuil de balcon .... 12 fr.

Bernheim Jeune, 25, Bd de la Madeleine
Durand, 4, Place de la Madeleine
Povolozky, 13, Rue Bonaparte
Au Sans Pareil, 37, Avenue Kléber
Six, 5, Avenue Lovendal
Paul Guillaume, 59, Rue la Boétie
Librairie Mornay, 37, Bd Montparnasse
Paul Rosenberg, 21, Rue la Boétie
et au Théâtre Michel. Tél. Gut. 63-30.

A page from *Bezette Stad* (Occupied City) by the Flemish poet Paul van Ostaijen, Antwerp, 1921.

hebben scheppen lantaarns fluweel rondom

d a n s e n d e k r a n s

donkerte om

l i c h t

trems scheppen om zich hun duisternis

meeschuivende duisternis met licht

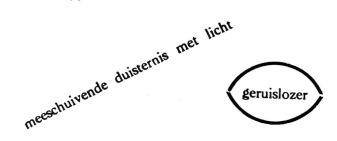
geruislozer

zinnen simultaan

het oor hoort - het geruisloze - dat
het oog Ziet

geruisloosheid lichtbeweging in mist

fluweel

Cover of the first edition of *Bezette Stad*,
designed by Oscar Jespers.

Jozef Peeters, Belgium, 1921.

on the Dadaist journal *Merz*, published in Hanover; and he contributed to the Dutch review *de Stijl*, edited by Theo van Doesburg. Lissitzky's influence accelerated the pace at which new conceptions in graphic design were adopted by publishers and advertisers, and within a few months of arriving in Berlin he had emerged as one of the dominant figures in the development of modern design. Mayakovsky's *For reading out loud*, which Lissitsky designed about the end of 1922, is an outstanding example of his imaginative and creative approach to book design and a landmark in the history of twentieth-century typography.

In the autumn of 1922 van Doesburg invited Lissitzky, Moholy-Nagy, Hans Richter, and some other proponents of Constructivism who were living in Germany to participate in a conference at Weimar, where he was then living and where the Bauhaus had been established some three years earlier. There, to their surprise – since most of them did not then know that van Doesburg, under the pseudonym of I. K. Bonset, was also an active Dadaist – the Constructivists were met by Hans Arp, Tristan Tzara, Kurt Schwitters, and other members of the Dada movement. Though the encounter was distasteful to many of the younger Constructivists, who regarded Dadaism as a negative influence, the Weimar meeting revealed some of the positive facets of Dadaism and helped to establish a bridge between the major movements.

In 1914, shortly before the outbreak of war, the distinguished Belgian Art Nouveau architect, Henry van de Velde, who was then principal of the Weimar School of Arts and Crafts, handed his resignation to the Grand Duke of Saxe-Weimar and recommended Walter Gropius, who was then 31, as one of three possible successors. Gropius had recently attracted attention as the architect of the factory for the 1914 Werkbund exhibition in which, as in his design for the Fagus factory three years earlier, he had used glass and steel in an entirely original way. The Grand Duke, however, decided to close the school and dismiss the staff, and it was not until after the war, and following prolonged negotiations, that Gropius's appointment was confirmed. By then Ducal rule had ended and it was decided to amalgamate two schools, the Grossherzogliche Kunstgewerbeschule and the Grossherzogliche Hochschule für Bildende Kunst, and in March 1919 Gropius was authorized to rename the combined schools 'Staatliches Bauhaus'.

Gropius defined the new school's objectives in a manifesto which he published in German newspapers in April: 'The complete building is the final aim of the visual arts

. . . Architects, painters and sculptors must recognize anew the composite character of a building as an entity . . . the artist is an exalted craftsman . . . *proficiency in his craft is essential to every artist*. Therein lies a source of creative imagination.' The Bauhaus programme was designed to eliminate the barriers which existed between artist, architect, craftsman, and industry, and it attracted students from all over Germany, from all social classes, and of widely different ages and experience, including many who had fought in the war.

The school's orientation was clouded, however, and its early development confused by Gropius's first three appointments to the teaching staff. Johannes Itten, who had opened a private art school in Vienna in 1915 and whose teaching methods there Gropius admired, was brought in to conduct the six-month preliminary course which all students were obliged to take before embarking upon specialized training in one of the workshops. Other vacancies were filled by the painter Lionel Feininger and the sculptor Gerhard Marcks, both of whom were Expressionists and members of the Novembergruppe, a romantic protest movement. Marcks was then relatively unknown, but the appointment of Feininger, whose revolutionary ideas on painting were heresy to the local academicians, immediately soured Gropius's relations with the Weimar bureaucracy. As a result of these appointments Expressionism became the dominant influence at the Bauhaus during its first two years and drove a wedge between Bauhaus theory and practice, but it was especially Itten's devotion to self-expression and to obscure cults and metaphysical speculation that was to provoke the first ideological crisis.

In theory the Bauhaus and de Stijl had similar aims, and about the end of 1920 van Doesburg, who had met Gropius in Berlin some months earlier, decided to go to Weimar to establish direct contact with the Bauhaus. But upon his arrival in Weimar van Doesburg was alarmed and dismayed to discover Itten's powerful influence in the school and the departure from aesthetic clarity which resulted from Itten's philosophy and the emphasis he placed upon intuitive solutions. Gropius and van Doesburg were both seeking to create an acceptable environment for man in an industrialized society through the marriage of art and industry. Gropius considered craft training important not as an end in itself, but as a means to an end, a way of achieving 'an affinity with industry' and of establishing contact with contemporary production problems. But he believed above all that the Bauhaus should avoid creating or imposing a style and that every student should have the opportunity to develop his own creative individuality.

Fernand Léger, Paris, 1919. (The
original of this composition is in three
colours: yellow, red and dark blue.)

What Van Doesburg labelled 'the caprice of Expressionism' is apparent in this title page of a Bauhaus publication designed by Lionel Feininger in 1921, and in the following two works by Itten and Röhl.

Johannes Itten, 1921. A five-colour
lithograph from the first Bauhaus
Portfolio.

Peter Röhl's design for a Bauhaus
programme, 1921.

Gropius recognized the importance of de Stijl achievements but was opposed to van Doesburg's dogmatic insistence upon the need to adopt a tightly defined geometrically based and impersonal style.

Gropius's lukewarm reception, however, did not deter van Doesburg from settling in Weimar, and his home quickly became a meeting place for Bauhaus students and for some members of the teaching staff. In this way, although an outsider, van Doesburg was able to exert great influence on the school, and the impact of his ideas soon became apparent, especially in Bauhaus typography and furniture design. His presence in Weimar undoubtedly encouraged Gropius to combat Itten's influence in the school and accelerated the movement away from what van Doesburg called 'the caprice of Expressionism' towards Constructivism.

By the beginning of 1921 Itten's negative approach had begun to cause Gropius great concern and he decided to curb Itten's influence by making a number of administrative changes. Paul Klee, who brought an intellectual and highly analytical approach to teaching, had joined the staff at the end of 1920, and Gropius now sought to persuade Wassily Kandinsky to return from Russia. Kandinsky agreed, and in the spring of 1922 he was appointed *Formmeister* in the department of mural decoration. Early the following year, when Itten resigned following a further disagreement with Gropius over the conduct of the preliminary course, Laszlo Moholy-Nagy, who was then 28, was appointed to replace him. Together Klee, Kandinsky, and Moholy-Nagy gave Bauhaus teaching a new impetus and students a clear and positive goal. The arrival of Moholy-Nagy, especially, was of the greatest importance to the future development of the Bauhaus. Young, extrovert, and enthusiastic, he was quick to recognize the potentialities of Gropius's programme and to grasp its significance for the future of typography, photography, and the cinema as well as for painting and architecture.

Against a background of inflation and mounting political unrest, relations between the Bauhaus and the Thuringian Government were, however, rapidly deteriorating, and in the summer of 1923 the school was compelled by the authorities to mount an exhibition of its work. Gropius was reluctant to make such a demonstration so soon, but the task of arranging the exhibition united staff and students in a common project and revealed how much had been achieved, despite internal friction and external agitation, in just four years. The exhibition was visited by some 15,000 people and

The influence of Constructivism is clear in this design produced by Joost Schmidt as a student of the Weimar Bauhaus in 1924. (Schmidt was appointed to the teaching staff when the Bauhaus moved to Dessau the following year.)

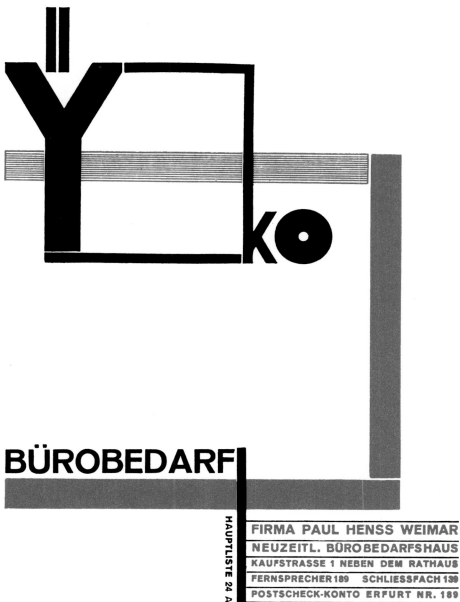

BÜROBEDARF

HAUPTLISTE 24 A

FIRMA PAUL HENSS WEIMAR
NEUZEITL. BÜROBEDARFSHAUS
KAUFSTRASSE 1 NEBEN DEM RATHAUS
FERNSPRECHER 189   SCHLIESSFACH 130
POSTSCHECK-KONTO ERFURT NR. 189

KUNSTVEREIN JENA

PRINZESSINNENSCHLÖSSCHEN
GEÖFFNET: SONNABENDS 3—5, SONNTAGS 11—1 UHR
AUSSER DER ZEIT FÜHRUNG DURCH DEN HAUSMEISTER

**14. DEZEMBER 1924
BIS 11. JANUAR 1925**

OSKAR SCHLEMMER

GEMÄLDE   ZEICHNUNGEN   BÜHNENENTWÜRFE   FIGURINEN

Invitation card designed by Walter
Dexel, 1924.

Da forchte
sich der Hut-Schapo
da forchte sich der Frack
da forchte sich der
ACH so
schöne Spitzenschal
B ACH

From the children's book *Die Scheuche* (The Scarecrow) by Schwitters, Van Doesburg, and Käte Steinitz, Hanover, 1925.

Left:
Front and back cover, greatly reduced, of a special issue of the periodical *Wendingen*, devoted to the work of Diego Rivera. The design is by Vilmos Huszar, one of the original members of the de Stijl group. Amsterdam, 1929. (The original is in red and green.)

widely praised by critics in Europe and America. But the following year, a few months after the election of a new, conservative regime, the Government of Thuringia gave cautionary notice to all Bauhaus staff and attempted to impose conditions which Gropius and his staff rejected. Gropius then entered into negotiations with the mayor of Dessau, Dr Fritz Hesse, and in April 1925 Bauhaus staff and students moved with some of their equipment to temporary premises in that small provincial town. There, during the next eighteen months, with Hesse's support, Gropius was able to build a new technical school with workshops, library and auditorium, a residential wing with twenty-eight studio-apartments for students, and a separate group of houses for the teaching staff.

Following the move from Weimar, Gropius reorganized the school and modified the curriculum. Six former students were appointed teachers and a typography workshop was established under Herbert Bayer. At Dessau, Gropius arranged that the preliminary course should be run jointly by Moholy-Nagy and Josef Albers. Marcel Breuer was put in charge of the furniture workshop and Joost Schmidt was made responsible for the plastic workshop.

By the end of 1926, housed in Gropius's new buildings and surrounded by furniture

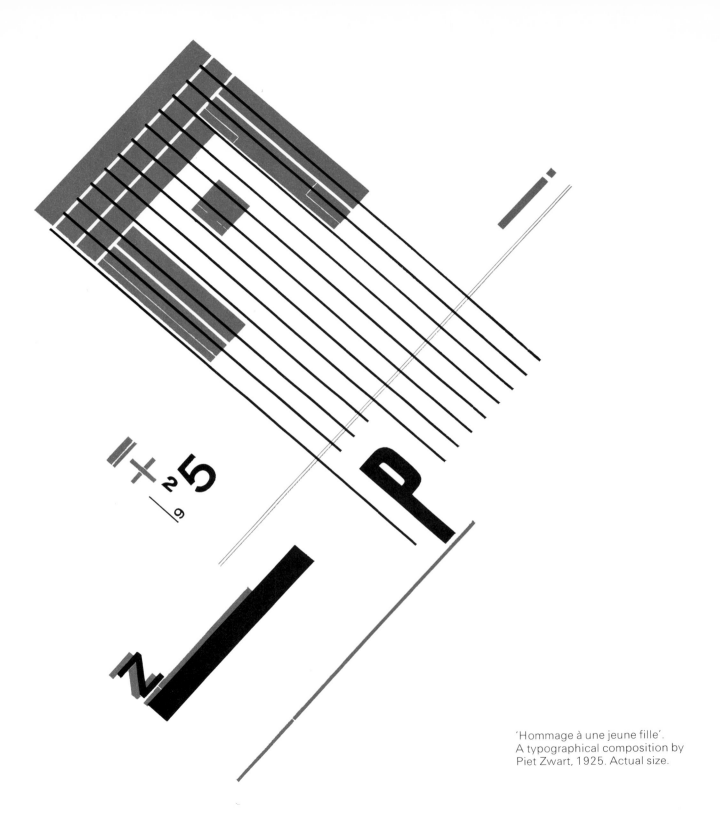

'Hommage à une jeune fille'.
A typographical composition by
Piet Zwart, 1925. Actual size.

One of several typographical compositions by Karel Teige for a book of poems by Konstantin Biebl, published in Prague in 1928

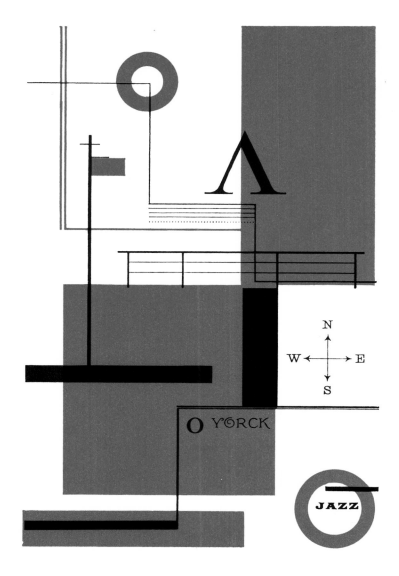

John Heartfield, Berlin, 1917. Pages from the large-format newspaper *Neue Jugend* published by Der Malik, a publishing house established by John Heartfield and his brother Helmut Herzfelde in 1917.

and decorations of their own creation, Bauhaus staff and students seemed at last to have discovered their true identity. The months following the move from Weimar were filled with intense activity and the designs which then poured out of the workshops were linked by a recognizable style. The impress of de Stijl and Constructivist ideas was unmistakable, but it is equally apparent in the designs of that period that the Bauhaus style was the result not of unquestioning acceptance of preconceived ideas – which Gropius had so strongly opposed – but of the sensitive and rational application of certain clearly understood principles to which all had contributed. What emerged from the Bauhaus at Dessau was not a string of fashionable cliches, but a clear statement made with quiet authority in a new and rich vocabulary.

In Poland between 1917 and 1919 a group of Expressionist writers and painters had published a magazine called *Zdrój* (Source) which echoed many of the metaphysical ideas voiced by the German Expressionists in Herwarth Walden's magazine *Der Sturm*. About the same period another group of artists, composed of a mixture of Cubists and Futurists, created a movement they named Formism. In Warsaw, at the end of 1920, the poets Anatol Stern and Aleksander Wat, who were the leading Polish Futurists, published *GGA* which contained some word-making experiments and a manifesto

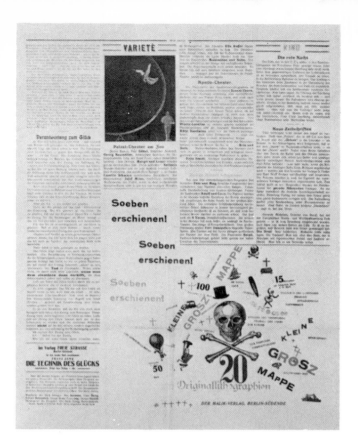

which proclaimed 'art is science'. A few months later Lissitzky visited Warsaw and gave a lecture which was attended by Henryk Berlewi, who was then 26. For Berlewi this encounter with Lissitzky was decisive, and in 1922 he went to Berlin where he began working on a series of experiments which led to 'Mechano-faktura'. Berlewi considered modern art to be full of 'illusionistic traps' which he sought to avoid by introducing a system of mechanical techniques. His works, which have been described as 'mechanical constructivism', are essentially two-dimensional graphic compositions built up of simple geometrical and reproduceable elements. In most of his constructions he employed typographical material and the colours red, black, and white. In 1924, together with Wat and Stanislaw Brucz, he established an advertising agency in Warsaw, called Reklama Mechano, and the powerful typographic designs produced by Berlewi at that time are uncompromising demonstrations of his conviction that 'advertising must adhere to the same principles as modern production'. 1924 also saw the launching in Warsaw of the first issue of the *avant-garde* magazine *Blok*, which united Polish artists of many different groups. *Blok* was concerned with the 'aesthetics of maximal economy', and among its many contributors were Mies van der Rohe, van Doesburg, Lissitzky, Arp, Malevich, Oud, Stern, Szczuka, Berlewi, and Strzeminski.

A 'Vortograph' by Alvin Langdon
Coburn, 1917; a 'Schadograph' by the
Zurich Dadaist, Christian Schad, 1918;
a 'Rayogram' by the American Dadaist,
Man Ray, 1921; and a 'Photogram' by
Laszlo Moholy-Nagy, 1922.

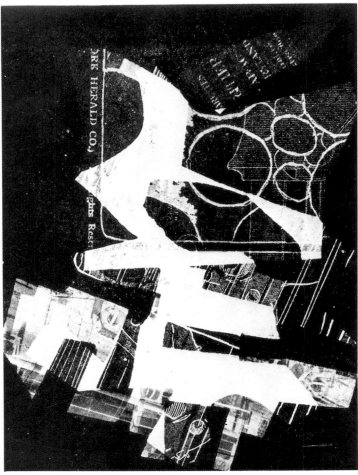

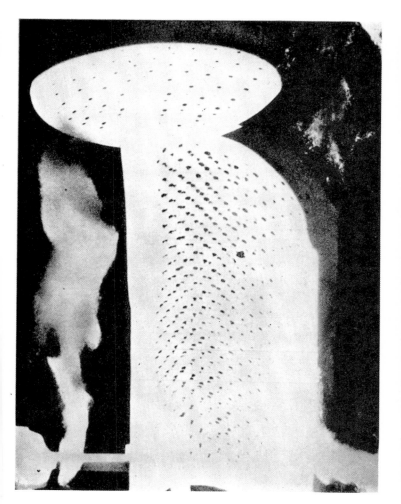

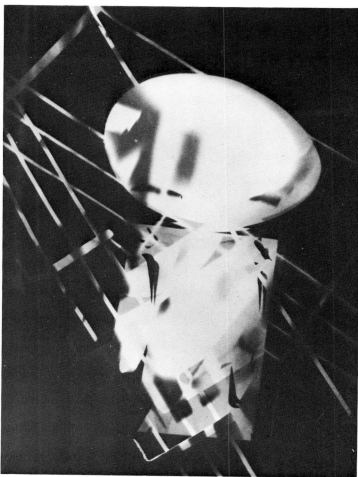

A montage by Raoul Hausmann and one
by Kurt Schwitters, both of 1920.

A photomontage entitled *The multi-millionaire* by Hannah Höch, 1920.

About the same time as Berlewi was experimenting with printers' material in order to produce pictures 'independent of caprice' Hendrik Werkman, a printer in Groningen in northern Holland, was quietly investigating the possibilities of using the materials he found in his workshop to create abstract compositions of form and colour in which chance and accident played a part. In these early *druksels*, as he called them, which were lightly printed on coarse paper, Werkman explored the interior shapes of letters and, in doing so, revealed the significance of texture and the potentialities of paper as a positive element in graphic design. Werkman's imaginative use of paper is also demonstrated in the series of typographical experiments he published for his friends, from 1923 onwards, under the title of *the next call*.

Many early examples of modern typography are manifestos and other publications issued by the designers themselves, but in Holland in the mid-1920's two men

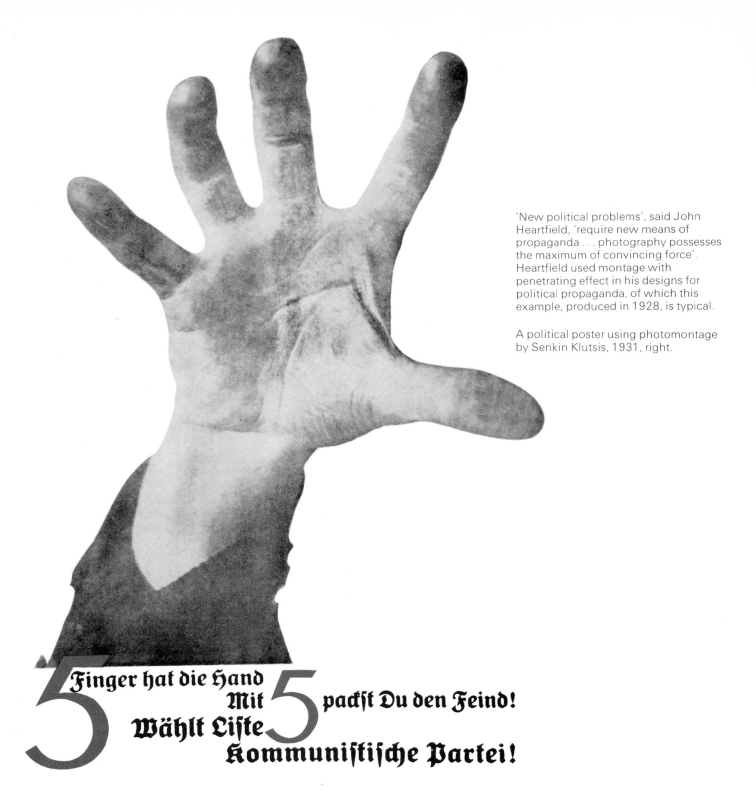

'New political problems', said John Heartfield, 'require new means of propaganda . . . photography possesses the maximum of convincing force'. Heartfield used montage with penetrating effect in his designs for political propaganda, of which this example, produced in 1928, is typical.

A political poster using photomontage by Senkin Klutsis, 1931, right.

5 Finger hat die Hand
Mit 5 packst Du den Feind!
Wählt Liste
Kommunistische Partei!

A cover design for *Broom* magazine by
Enrico Prampolini, 1923.

especially were responsible for applying to commercial advertising the principles of de
Stijl and of Constructivism: Piet Zwart and Paul Schuitema. They did so without
making concessions, and Zwart's press advertisements for NKF and Schuitema's
designs for Berkel are among the most vigorous and penetrating early examples of the
new typography. Zwart and Schuitema devised both the message and the technique
used to convey that message. They utilized the types they found in the printer's cases,
but they liberated them from their horizontal straitjacket. When they used photographs
of photomontage, as they often did, they did so not as an embellishment, but in order
to make the message immediate and international.

In Germany, in October 1925, modern typography was introduced to a wide audience
of practical printers for the first time through the publication of a special issue of the
printing trade journal, *Typographische Mitteilungen*. Written by Jan Tschichold, who
was then 23, this publication established Tschichold as an ardent and persuasive
advocate of asymmetrical typography. In his practical work during the late 'twenties

An early Polish photomontage, by
Mieczyslaw Szczuka, published in *Blok*
No.5, 1924, opposite.

Cover for the Hungarian journal *MA* No.5, by Lajos Kassák, 1924.

A cover design by Strzemiński for Tadeusz Peiper's *Szósta! Szósta!* Warsaw, 1925.

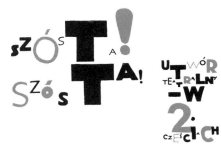

A typographical composition by Teresa
Zarnower, Warsaw, 1924;

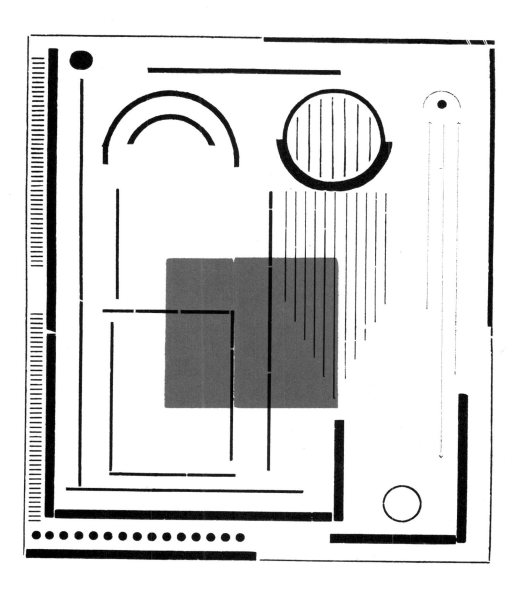

Two *mechano-faktura* constructions by Henryk Berlewi, 1922. The originals are in red and black.

Henryk Berlewi, Warsaw, 1924. Cover
and pages from a booklet *Reklama
Mechano*. Slightly reduced. The original
was printed on yellow paper.

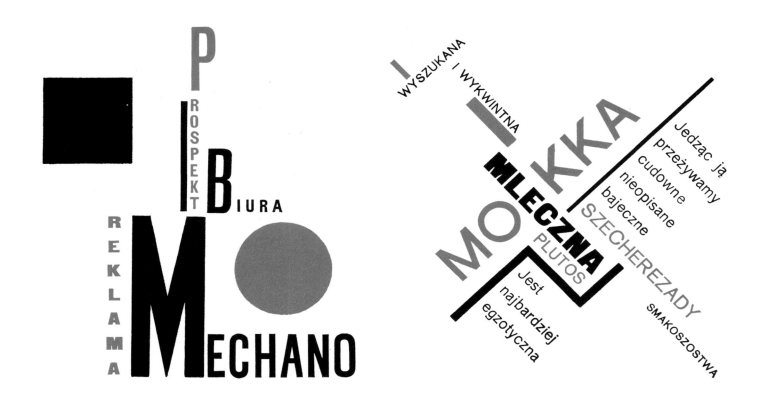

and early 'thirties, using the new machine-composition series of typefaces that were
then becoming available, Tschichold demonstrated the subtlety, the precision, and the
elegance of which modern typography is capable. But in the articles and books which
he wrote during this period, Tschichold attempted to formulate a narrow definition of
modern typography. The simple rules-of-thumb which he then proffered were quickly
grasped by compositors and printers and, at first, Tschichold's dogmatic assertion of
his ideas served to quicken the pace at which asymmetric typography was adopted by
the German printing industry. However, in relation to the emerging techniques of
reproduction and new needs and opportunities in publishing and in advertising,

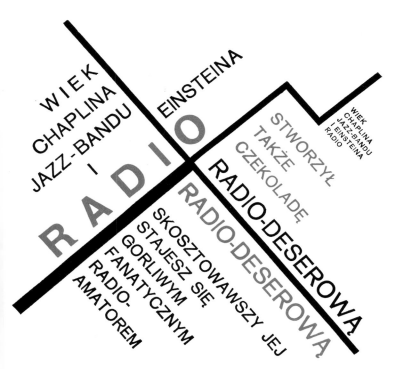

Tschichold's attempt to codify modern typography in this way was neither necessary nor relevant. It was an endeavour which contradicted the spirit of modern typography and one which, if it had succeeded, would have done much to vitiate it and to diminish its essential vitality and flexibility.

The fundamental difference between traditional, centred and modern typography is that the one is passive and the other is active, though not necessarily aggressive. Asymmetry and contrast provide the basis of modern typography.

At the beginning of this century most printing was still done by letterpress from metal type. The Futurists, however, as we have seen, had successfully thrust off the horizontal discipline which the invention of printing from movable types had imposed upon the page. Many years in advance of the development of methods of photo-typesetting and the invention of dry transfer lettering they had produced compositions which were fundamentally non-linear in conception and which, even with today's resources, can hardly be surpassed as demonstrations of typographical freedom and flexibility. As writers and artists, they had looked at the page with the eyes of the recipient rather than, as the printer had done, with those of the producer. In their determination to achieve printed images that were dynamic, the Futurists had presented their printers with extraordinary demands, and they had persuaded, cajoled or bullied their compositors into remarkable feats of ingenuity in the manipulation of typographical material.

In his *Manifesto of Futurism* Marinetti had proclaimed the importance of contrast. In the early works of the Futurists, and also in those of the Dadaists, contrast was achieved through the combination of a wide – and, sometimes, a wild – variety of types that were markedly different in weight and size as well as design. The departure from symmetry and horizontality imbued these composition with a sense of movement and vitality, but it was the Constructivists and de Stijl who explored the spatial opportunities of asymmetrical design and who first clearly indicated how tension, impact, drama and excitement, on the one hand, and clarity and eloquence, on the other, could be introduced into the printed page through the free but sensitive distribution of space and the interplay of type and paper. The work of the Constructivists and de Stijl also showed how colour could be employed as a fundamental design element rather than as a mere embellisment added as an afterthought.

The early typographical works of Lissitzky, Schwitters, van Doesburg and Zwart are animated by the imaginative use of contrast in the utilization of space, by the dramatic distribution of black and white, and by the skilful exploration of colour. Their pages vibrate from the impact of powerful and sometimes surprising typographical juxtapositions. With care and discrimination they selected from the wood and metal types they found in their printers' cases those letters that were sympathetic to their conceptions. When the letter-shapes they required were not readily available they did not hesitate to construct them out of metal rules and ornaments and other odds and

A cover design by Szczuka for the magazine *Blok*. Warsaw, 1926. The original is in red and black.

Overleaf:
A double spread from *Europa*, a poem by Anatol Stern, designed by Mieczyslaw Szczuka and published in Warsaw in 1929. Szczuka had prepared these designs in 1927, shortly before his death in a mountaineering accident at the age of 29.

tu trzeba miljonow

stalowych narzędzi

wszystkie Timesy świata

nie starczą na jeden wiersz

to trzeba śpiewać wiekami

odnotować

wszystkie eksplozje

atomów

obnażyć

sejsmograf

podświadomości

człowiek ułożony

z zapałek

i ten 3000 letni

z jaskini madziarskiej

to rozłączeni bracia

epoka kamienia

wszystko jedno jakiego

przecina się z naszym
        żelazo-betonem
to wyścig epok
zawsze to samo
wysokie
morderstwo
cywilizacji
ekstaza zmysłowości
skrzywiony natężeniem
mózg

XX wiek
to haarman

pożerający swoje miłości!
intelektualizm
to sadyzm psychiczny
nie przekształcajcie życia
w walkę typów logicznych
wielka terapeutyka
przyszłości —
trening żarłoctwa się zbliża!

tradycja i ciągłość —
to wielkości urojone
wynalazco
jesteś synem przypadku!

śpieszymy do wielkiej
reakcji swobody
ukoronowanej 20 wiekowym
przymusem
jedyną realną stacją jest ta
której brak
w żółtym rozkładzie jazdy
pozwólcie mi
        spocząć na chwilę
przeciąć kable
swej wrażliwości

ten zielony kieł trawki
ściśniętej dwiema
        płytami trotuaru
ten wyrywający się rozbitek
na pokratkowanym
kamiennym
atlantyku
to goniec śmierci
patrzcie
trzyma w wątłej ręce
góry
doliny
przecięte rzekami
jodły
jawory

Title page by Ladislav Sutnar, Prague, 1931.

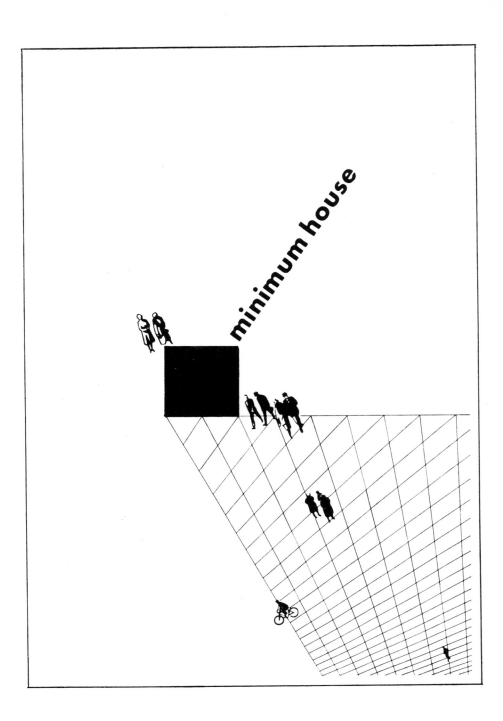

Exhibition poster by Max Bill, Zurich,
1931. Original in brown and black.

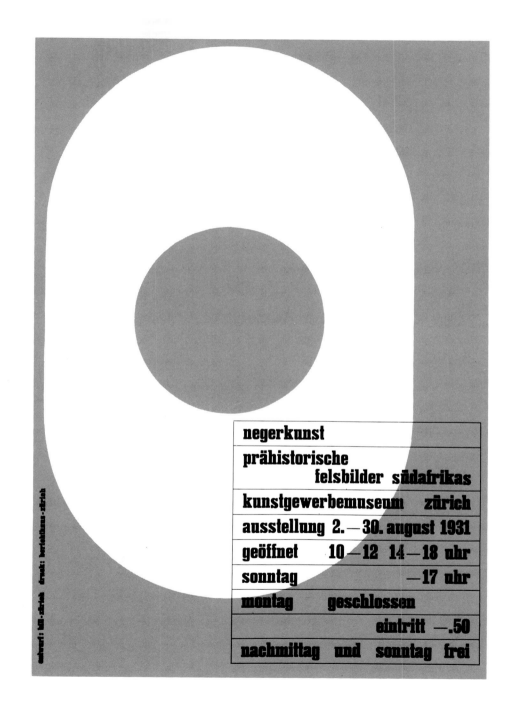

Herbert Bayer, 1926: poster design.

ends ferreted out of forgotten corners of the composing room. The choice of typefaces in these early works was, however, subjective and quite uninhibited by the theories that were later to assume such importance at the Dessau Bauhaus, and to determine the design of much printing produced in Germany during the late 'twenties and early 'thirties.

After 1925, Herbert Bayer, at the Bauhaus, and Jan Tschichold, at the Munich School, both energetically encouraged the use of sanserif types and both designed geometrically-constructed sanserif alphabets. Sanserif types reflected the notion of 'beauty in utility', which had become the pivot of Bauhaus experiments, and they also permitted more subtle typographical contrasts of visual weight. Bayer argued strongly in favour of a single alphabet – 'why should we write and print in two alphabets? we do not speak a capital A and a small a' – and after the move to Dessau the Bauhaus began to abandon the use of capital letters in its publications. Both Tschichold and Schwitters experimented with phonetic alphabets.

The debates about typefaces, about serifs, and other typographical minutiae which, during the late 'twenties and subsequently, have often surrounded modern typography, have sometimes obscured its fundamental characteristics and the advantages, in terms of visual fluency and clarity, which flow from the imaginative use of contrast and asymmetry. This book records some of the achievements of those pioneers of modern typography who, in a period of war and revolution and of political and economic instability, with slender resources but fierce determination and unwavering dedication, created a new and richer visual vocabulary.

El Lissitzky's letterhead, original in red
and black.

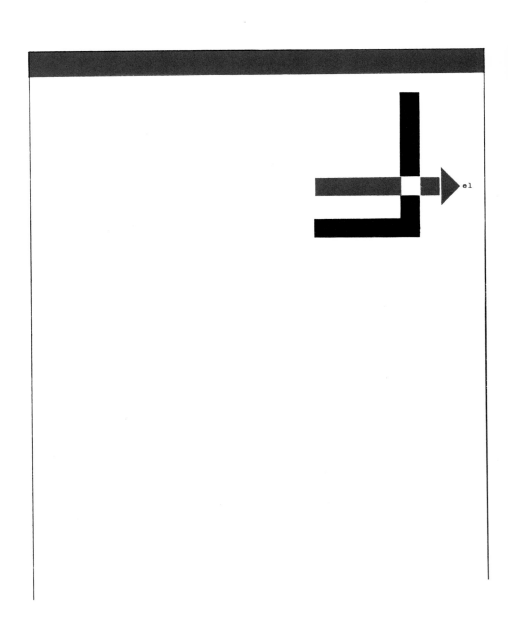

Lazar Markovitch Lissitzky was born at Polshinok in the province of Smolensk in November 1890. He grew up in Vitebsk and, later, attended high school in Smolensk. In 1909, at the age of 19, he left Russia to study at the Darmstadt school of engineering and architecture. He made his first visit to Paris in the summer of 1911 and went on an extensive walking tour of northern Italy the following year, drawing and studying Italian architecture.

He graduated from the Darmstadt school in the summer of 1914. When war broke out he was able to return to Russia only with great difficulty, through Switzerland and the Balkans. In Moscow he worked as an architectural assistant, first with Felikovsky and later with Klein. In the spring of 1917 he produced the first of a series of Jewish picture books.

Following the Revolution, Marc Chagall had become principal of the Vitebsk art school, and in 1919 he appointed Lissitzky professor of architecture. There, under the influence of the Suprematist painter, Kasimir Malevich, who was one of his colleagues in the school, Lissitzky began to work on the experimental designs he called 'Prouns'. These, his first non-objective works, were a synthesis of Suprematist and Constructivist elements and Lissitzky described them as 'the interchange station between painting and architecture'. He soon began to incorporate typographical elements in his paintings and at the same time to design posters and book covers. His arresting civil war poster 'Beat the Whites with the Red Wedge' is from this period, and this was followed by the Suprematist story *Two Squares* designed in Vitebsk in 1920 and published in Berlin (and also, in a Dutch version, in *de Stijl*) two years later.

In 1921, after a brief period in Moscow teaching at the new Vkhutemas art school under Tatlin, Lissitzky returned to Germany. Berlin was then full of Russians – Pasternak, Mayakovsky, Archipenko, Gabo, Antoine Pevsner, Altman, and Ehrenburg were among the Russian artistic intelligentsia who were there. Lissitzky and Ehrenburg decided to collaborate in the production of a tri-lingual periodical devoted to ' the new objectivity' and the first issue of *Veshch/Gegenstand/Objet* appeared early in 1922. This publication and the highly developed printing facilities which were available to him in Germany provided Lissitzky with a splendid opportunity to implement and develop his typographical ideas.

For Lissitzky, a man of fantastic energy and persistence, 1922 was a year of

El Lissitsky, 1927
Cover for Alexander Tairoff's *Das entfesselte Theater*, Gustav Kiepenheuer Verlag, Potsdam.
Greatly reduced.
Original in red and black.

tremendous activity. He had been commissioned to design a Constructivist room in the big Russian Art Exhibition at the Galerie van Diemen in Berlin and later that year he accompanied the exhibition to Amsterdam. He participated in the meeting attended by Constructivists and Dadaists in Weimar. He wrote a number of articles and lectured widely. He made visits to the Bauhaus and had frequent meetings with van Doesburg, Moholy-Nagy, and Schwitters. He designed covers for the American magazine *Broom*, edited by Harold Loeb and Matthew Josephson, and for Skhlovsky's *Zoo, Letters not about love*. He prepared illustrations and a cover design for Ilya Ehrenburg's *Six Tales with Easy Endings*. And at the end of that year Mayakovsky asked Lissitzky to design and illustrate his book *For reading out loud*, which was to be printed in Germany for publication by the State Publishing House in Moscow.

Lissitzky continued to work at the same feverish pitch throughout most of the following year, but in October he was taken ill with pneumonia, and a few weeks later pulmonary tuberculosis was diagnosed. In February 1924 he entered a sanatorium at Orselina, near Locarno, and from there he continued to work on the special number of *Merz* which Schwitters had invited him to edit and to prepare designs for a series of advertisements for Pelikan. In Switzerland he embarked on a series of photographic experiments, and during the summer he began work with Hans Arp on *The isms of art*, which the Zurich publisher Eugen Rentsch had agreed to publish. The following winter, however, he was again very ill and also beset by financial difficulties. In February the news reached him that his sister had committed suicide. He decided to return home. He remained in Russia until June 1926 when he returned to Germany to design an exhibition room as part of the International Art Exhibition in Dresden, and afterwards went to stay with Mart Stam in Holland. During this visit to Germany Lissitzky proposed to the German widow of Paul Küppers, Sophie, and at the beginning of 1927 she joined him in Moscow where they were married on 27 January. Lissitzky, now deeply immersed in the problems of exhibition design, was commissioned to design the 1927 Union Polygraphic Exhibiton in Moscow and the success of this led to his appointment to control the design of the large Soviet Pavilion at the International Press Exhibition, *Pressa*, in Cologne in the spring of 1928. During the next two years he designed three other important Soviet exhibitions in Germany – at Stuttgart, Dresden, and Leipzig.

During the early 'thirties Lissitzky's health deteriorated rapidly and periods of intense activity were disrupted by spells of illness. He died near Moscow in December 1941.

ПОД РЕДАКЦИЕЙ ЭЛ ЛИСИЦКОГО И ИЛЬИ ЭРЕНБУРГА

GEGENSTAND — INTERNATIONALE RUNDSCHAU DER KUNST DER GEGENWART

ВЕЩЬ

МЕЖДУНАРОДНОЕ ОБОЗРЕНИЕ СОВРЕМЕННОГО ИСКУССТВА

OBJET — REVUE INTERNATIONALE DE L'ART MODERNE

№ 1-2

БЕРЛИН МАРТ—АПРЕЛЬ 1922

PUBLIÉE SOUS LA DIRECTION DE EL LISSITZKY ET ELIE EHRENBURG

DIE BLOCKADE RUSSLANDS GEHT IHREM ENDE ENTGEGEN,—

das ERSCHEINEN des

„GEGENSTANDES"

ist auch ein Anzeichen dafür, daß der Austausch von Erfahrungen, von Errungenem, von „Gegenständen" zwischen jungen russischen und westeuropäischen Meistern begonnen hat. Sieben Jahre gesonderten Seins haben gezeigt, daß die Gemeinsamkeit der Aufgaben und Ziele der Kunst in den verschiedenen Ländern nicht auf Zufall beruht, auch nicht Dogma oder Mode, sondern eine in sich selber beruhende Eigenschaft der gereiften Menschheit ist. Die Kunst ist von nun ab, bei Wahrung aller lokalen Eigentümlichkeiten und Symptome, international. Die Begründer einer neuen Meisterschaft befestigen sichere Fugen zwischen Rußland, das die gewaltige Revolution durchlebte, und dem Westen mit seiner jammervollen Blaumontagsstimmung nach dem Kriege; hierbei übergehen sie alle Unterscheidungen psychologischer, wirtschaftlicher, völkischer Art. Der „GEGENSTAND" ist das Bindestück zwischen zwei benachbarten Laufgräben.

Wir stehen im Beginn einer großen schopferischen Epoche. Natürlich sind Reaktion und bourgeoiser Starrsinn

LE BLOCUS DE LA RUSSIE TOUCHE À SA FIN

L'APPARITION de

„L'OBJET"

est l'un des indices de l'échange d'experiences, de réussites d'objets qui commence à se faire entre les jeunes artisans de Russie et d'Occident. Sept ans d'existence séparée, ont prouvé que la communauté d'aspirations et de voies, dans le domaine artistique, entre différents pays, n'est pas un effet du hasard, une mode, mais bien la propriété inévitable d'une humanité mûrie.

L'art, aujourd'hui, est international, tout en ayant conservé le caractère local des symptômes et des traits particuliers.

Les constructeurs de l'art nouveau, passant par-dessus les différences de psychologie, de mœurs et d'économie, établissent un lien solide entre la Russie, qui a subi la grande Révolution, et l'Occident avec son lundi - accablant.

„L'OBJET"

est la jonction de deux tranchées alliées. Nous assistons à la naissance d'une grande époque constructive. Il va de soi que la réaction et l'entêtement bourgeois sont encore grands partout, aussi bien en Europe que dans la

БЛОКАДА РОССИИ КОНЧАЕТСЯ

ПОЯВЛЕНИЕ

„ВЕЩИ"

один из признаков начинающегося обмена опытами, достижениями, вещами между молодыми мастерами России и Запада. Семь лет раздельного бытия показали, что общность заданий и путей искусства различных стран не случайность, не догма, не мода, но неизбежное свойство возмужалости человечества. Искусство ныне ИНТЕРНАЦИОНАЛЬНО, при всей локальности частных симптомов и черт. Между Россией, пережившей величайшую Революцию, и Западом, с его томительным послевоенным бездельником, минуя разность психологии, быта и экономики строит верный скреп

„ВЕЩЬ"

стык двух союзных окопов.

Мы присутствуем при начале великой СОЗИДАТЕЛЬНОЙ ЭПОХИ. Конечно реакция и мещанское упрямство сильны повсюду, и в Европе, и в единстве с устоев России Но все усилия староверов могут лишь замедлить процесс строительства новых форм бытия и мастерства. Дни разрушения, осады и подкопа, — позади. Вот почему

„ВЕЩЬ"

ECOUTEZ, CANAILLES

■ Cloués par ces lignes, ■ Restez muets ■ Ecoutez ces hurlements de loup ■ Qui ressemblent à peine à un poème! ■ Donnez ici ■ Le plus gros ■ Le plus chauve, ■ Prenez au collet et poussez le ■ Dans la boue et les comptes ■ Des Comités de l'aide aux affamés! ■ Regarde, ■ Tu vois ■ Derrière les chiffres nus... ■ Un coup de vent ■ Fort et doux ■ Enveloppe dans la neige ■ Des milliers ■ De millions de toits, ■ La neige ■ Cercueil des villages du Volga. ■ Les cheminées, ■ Les cierges. ■ Même les corbeaux ■ Disparaissent, ■ Ils sentent ■ Sous, fumante, ■ Arrive ■ Douce et nauséabonde, ■ L'odeur ■ Du fils, ■ Du père, ■ De la mère, ■ De la fille ■ Que l'on a rôti. ■ De qui est-ce le tour? ■ Il n'y aura pas de secours. ■ Séparés par la neige, ■ Pas de secours, ■ L'air est vide! ■ Pas de secours! ■ Sous les pieds, ■ Même le mortier ■ On le dévore! ■ Même les mauvaises herbes! ■ Non, ■ Pas de pain, ■ Il faut se rendre. ■ Pour dix provinces ■ Mesurez les tombes. ■ Vingt millions ■ Vingt, ■ Couchez-vous, ■ Mourez! ■ Mais seule, ■ Avec une tête de pain, ■ Même de folles malédictions, ■ Les cheveux neigeux des chemins ■ Tirés par le vent. ■ Sanglote la terre. ■ Du pain, ■ Un peu de pain! ■ Encore du pain! ■ Elle même, voyant la mort en face, ■ Ayant à manger, ■ Pour ne pas crever ■ La ville tend sa main ouvrière, ■ Une poignée de miette desséchée. ■ Du pain, ■ Un peu de pain, ■ Un peu de pain! ■ Les radio ■ Hurlent à toutes les frontières ■ Et comme réponse ■ Bêtises sur bêtises ■ Tombent dans les colonnes ■ Des journaux. ■ „Londres, ■ Banquet, ■ Présence du roi et de la reine ■ Qui bouffent ■ Ce qui pourrait rentrer ■ Dans une bauge tout en or!" ■ Soyez maudits! ■ Que ■ Pour votre tête couronnée ■ Des princesses, ■ Accourent les sauvages ■ Les anthropophages. ■ Que ■ Brûle sur le royaume ■ L'incendie des révoltes! ■ Que ■ Vos capitales ■ Soient brûlées ■ Tout entières! ■ Que ■ Des princes héritiers, ■ Des princesses, ■ Le manger ■ Se prépare ■ Dans des couronnes marmites! ■ „Paris, ■ Réunion du Parlement, ■ Rapport sur la famine ■ Par Fridjof Nansen". ■ On écoute en souriant ■ Comme un air de resignes! ■ Comme si on écoutait ■ Un ténor ■ Dans une romance à la mode ■ Soyez maudits! ■ Que ■ Pour l'éternité ■ Vous n'entendiez plus ■ La voix humaine! ■ Proletariat français ■ Hé! ■ Prends dans un nœud ■ Au lieu de drapeau ■ „Paris, ■ Washington, ■ Les fermiers ayant bouffé, ■ Avant bu, ■ Tellement ■ Qu'il leur faut ■ Une grue ■ Pour soulever leur panse! ■ Dans la mer ■ Le meilleur de superflu ■ De la fine farine, ■ Chauffent les locomotives ■ Avec du maïs!" ■ Soyez maudits! ■ Que ■ Vos rues ■ Soient pleines de révoltes, ■ Que, ■ trouvant ■ Les places les plus sensibles, ■ Sur le Nord ■ Et sur le Sud ■ De l'Amérique, ■ On joue de vos panses! ■ Comme des balles du foot-ball ■ „Berlin, ■ Les émigrés ressuscitent, ■ Leurs bandes sont satisfaites, ■ Avec les affamés ■ Ils se battent. ■ A Berlin, ■ Frisant sa moustache, ■ Marche, ave vante, ■ Le patriote russe. ■ Soyez maudits! ■ Dehors! ■ Eternellement! ■ Dégoûtez tout le monde ■ Par votre air de Judas, ■ Poursuivi par le son ■ De l'or français. ■ Soyez errante ■ Pour l'éternité! ■ Forêts russes, ■ Rassemblez-vous, ■ Chelsissez vos plus grands arbres, ■ Que leur image ■ Toujours pendue, ■ Se balance toute bleue ■ Contre le ciel! ■ Moscou, ■ La rassemblée se plaint: ■ „A l'Empire, ■ On fait des grimaces, ■ On y donne trente roubles ■ Qui ne marchent plus ■ Depuis 1918!" ■ Soyez maudits! ■ Que cela soit ainsi! ■ Que chaque bouchée avalée ■ Vous brûle l'estomac! ■ Qu'un biftek saignant ■ Se change en ciseaux ■ Et vous coupe les intestins! ■ Seront morts ■ Vingt millions d'hommes. ■ Au nom de tous ceux qui sont morts ■ Malédiction aujourd'hui! ■ Jusqu'à l'éternité ■ A ceux qui ont détourné ■ Leur gueule bouffie ■ Du Volga! ■ Cette parole n'est pas ■ Pour la panse remplie ■ Ni pour le trône du Tsar! ■ Dans un tel cœur ■ Les mots ne peuvent rien toucher. ■ Les touchent ■ Les lances des révolutions! ■ A vous ■ Petits atomes ■ D'une énorme armée, ■ Avec la force de qui ■ Avec la force ■ Jetée dans les sous-sol, ■ On fera sauter le monde ■ Des milliardaires! ■ A vous! ■ A vous! ■ Ces paroles-là! ■ Avec des chiffres kilométriques ■ Faites le compte des bourgeois! ■ Le jour viendra ■ De l'incendie universel ■ Purifiant et fumant, ■ Mettant sans dessus dessous ■ Les palais des riches! ■ Soyez aussi. ■ Soyez sans pitié, ■ A cette heure ■ Du châtiment!

Majakowsky.

все же, мог бы быть целесообразным. Однако писатель стремится одновременно усвоить французские настроения и „точки зрения" не говоря уже про условности. Если они могли бы остаться американцами (не в узком смысле этого слова) и приобрести французскую ясность и легкость выражения и стиля, было бы прекрасно, но писать плохие французские романы на хорошем английском языке — вряд ли имеет смысла. Парижская школа американской литературы могла бы принести большую пользу. Существует пропасть между Америкой и ее литературой. Это едва заметно на Восточном берегу Атлантического Океана, но ясно всем на Западном. Пропасть, отделяющая представителей труда интеллектуального от мускульного, которая обособляет писателей, должна быть заполнена, если американская литература призвана перестать быть лишь угнетением полов, негодных обмещанину. Наша цивилизация выше этого. Они отличаются от других тем, что работали без денег и друзей в кошмарной обстановке промышленной борьбы, от которой содрогаются американские писатели и она нравилась. Работа американских литераторов для них лишена всякого интереса, тогда как естественные продукты нашей цивилизации кажутся им чудом зла.

BERLIN 1922

OBJET

ВЕЩЬ

№3

GEGENSTAND

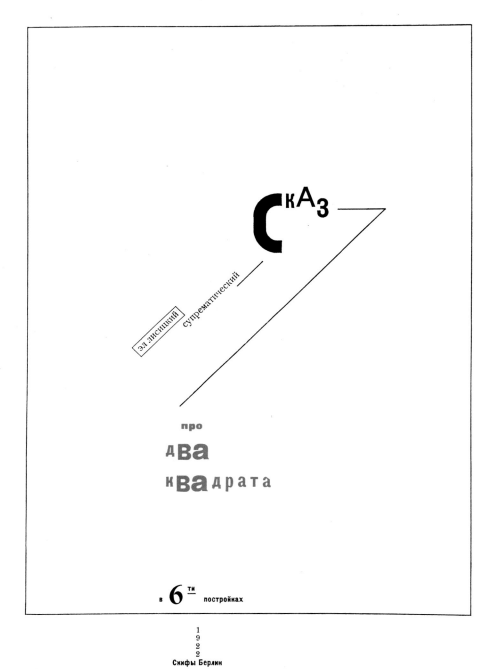

С^к**А**з

эл лисицкий супрематический

про

д**ва**

к**ва**драта

в **6**^{ти} постройках

1
9
2
2
Скифы Берлин

El Lissitzky, Vitebsk, 1920 (published Berlin 1922). Title-page, left, and double-page spread, below (reduced). from the Suprematist story *Two squares:* 'Don't read . . . get paper, rods, blocks . . . set them out, paint them, build'.

In this tale of two squares I have set out to formulate an elementary idea, using elementary means, so that children may find it a stimulus to active play and grown-ups enjoy it as something to look at. The action unrolls like a film . . .'

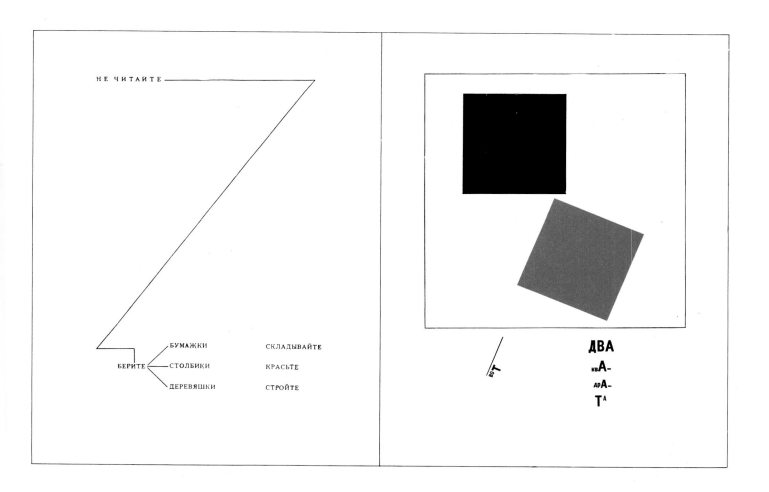

Title-page of the Dutch edition of *Two Squares*, published by De Stijl, 1922. Slightly reduced, original in red and black.

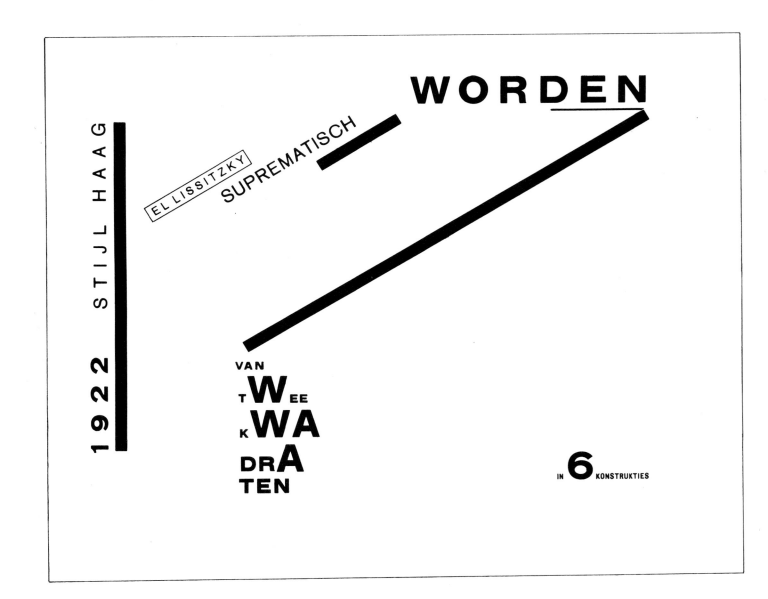

Cover of a leaflet for the Lissitzky
exhibition at the Galerie Nierendorf,
Berlin, in 1923.

77

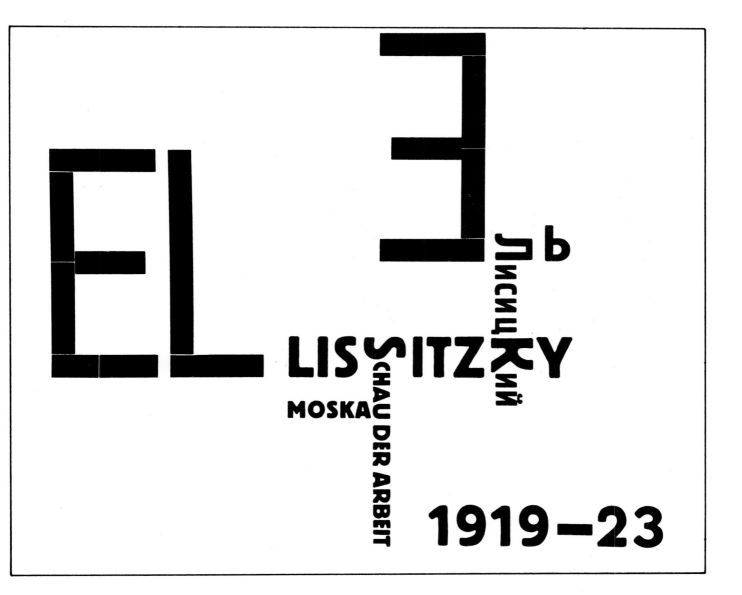

МАЯКОВСКИЙ

ДЛЯ ГОЛОСА

El Lissitzky, Berlin, 1923. Cover and pages from Mayakovsky's book of poems entitled *For reading out loud*. The original is printed in red and black and orange. The cover is reproduced actual size.

'To make it easier for the reader to find any particular poem, I use an alphabetical index. The book is created with the resources of the compositor's type-case alone. The possibilities of two-colour printing . . . have been exploited to the full. My pages stand in much the same relationship to the poems as an accompanying piano to a violin.'

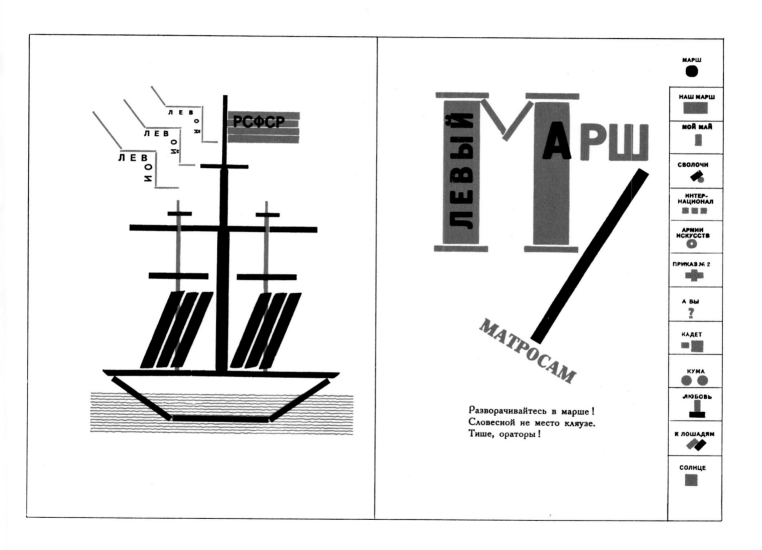

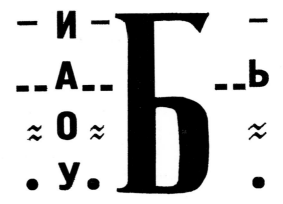

ХОрошее
Отношение
к ЛОШАДЯМ

Били копыта
пели будто:
— ГРИБ
ГРАБЬ
ГРОБ
ГРУБ —

К ЛОШАДЯМ

СОЛНЦЕ

8 MERZ 9

DIESES DOPPELHEFT IST ERSCHIENEN UNTER DER REDAKTION VON
EL LISSITZKY UND KURT SCHWITTERS

REDAKTION DES MERZVERLAGES
KURT SCHWITTERS, HANNOVER, WALDHAUSENSTR. 5"

TYPOGRAPHIE ANGEGEBEN VON EL LISSITZKY
K. SCHWITTERS
HERAUSGEBER

NATUR VON LAT. **NASCI**

D. I. WERDEN ODER ENT-

STEHEN HEISST ALLES,

WAS SICH AUS SICH

SELBST DURCH EIGENE

KRAFT ENTWICKELT

GESTALTET UND BEWEGT

KLEINER BROKHAUS

BAND 2, Nr. 8/9
APRIL
JULI
1924

Nature, du latin **NASCI** signifie devenir, provenir, c'est a dire tout ce qui par sa propre force, se développe, se forme, se meut.

82

El Lissitsky, 1925.
Title page and page from *The isms of art*.

III

DIE KUNSTISMEN

1924
1923
1922
1921
1920
1919
1918
1917
1916
1915
1914

HERAUSGEGEBEN VON EL LISSITZKY

UND HANS ARP

LES ISMES DE L'ART

1924
1923
1922
1921
1920
1919
1918
1917
1916
1915
1914

PUBLIÉS PAR EL LISSITZKY

ET HANS ARP

THE ISMS OF ART

1924
1923
1922
1921
1920
1919
1918
1917
1916
1915
1914

PUBLISHED BY EL LISSITZKY

AND HANS ARP

EUGEN RENTSCH VERLAG
ERLENBACH-ZÜRICH, MÜNCHEN UND LEIPZIG

1925

VIII

Die Gegenwart ist die Zeit der Analysen, das Resultat aller Systeme, die jemals entstanden sind. Zu unserer Demarkationsgrenze haben die Jahrhunderte die Zeichen gebracht. In ihnen werden wir Unvollkommenheiten erkennen, die zur Getrenntheit und Gegensätzlichkeit führten. Vielleicht werden wir davon nur das Gegensätzliche nehmen, um das System der Einheit aufzubauen. **MALEWITSCH.**

Le temps actuel est l'époque des analyses, le résultat de tous les systèmes qui aient jamais été établis. Ce sont des siècles qui ont apporté les signes de notre ligne de démarcation, nous y reconnaîtrons les imperfections qui menaient à la division et à la contradiction. Peut-être que nous n'en prendrons que les propos contradictoires pour construire notre système de l'unité. **MALEWITSCH.**

The actual time is the epoca of analyses, the result of all systems that ever were established. Centuries brought the signs to our line of demarcation. In them we shall recognise the imperfections that led to division and contradiction. Perhaps we hereof only shall take the contradictory to construct the system of unity. **MALEWITSCH.**

KUBISMUS

Das, was den Kubismus von der älteren Malerei unterscheidet, ist dieses: er ist nicht eine Kunst der Nachahmung, sondern eine Konzeption, welche strebt sich zur Schöpfung herauszuheben. **APOLLINAIRE.**

Statt der impressionistischen Raumillusion, die sich auf Luftperspektive und Farbennaturalismus gründet, gibt der Kubismus die schlichten, abstrahierten Formen in klaren Wesens- und Maßverhältnissen zueinander. **ALLARD.**

FUTURISMUS

Die Futuristen haben die Ruhe und Statik demoliert und das Bewegte, Dynamische gezeigt. Sie haben die neue Raumauffassung durch die Gegenüberstellung des Inneren und Außeren dokumentiert.

Die Geste ist für uns nicht mehr ein festgehaltener Augenblick der universalen Bewegtheit: sie ist entschieden die dynamische Sensation selbst und als solche verewigt. **BOCCIONI.**

EXPRESSIONISMUS

Aus Kubismus und Futurismus wurde der falsche Hase, das metaphysische deutsche Beefsteak, der Expressionismus gehackt.

CUBISME

Ce qui distingue le cubisme de la peinture précédente c'est qu'il n'est pas un art de l'imitation, mais une conception qui tend a s'élever en création. **APOLLINAIRE.**

Au lieu de l'illusion impressioniste de l'espace basée sur la perspective de l'air et le naturalisme des couleurs, le cubisme donne les formes simples et abstraites en leurs relations précises de caractère et de mesures. **ALLARD.**

FUTURISME

Les futuristes ont démoli la quiétude et la statique et démontré le mouvement, la dynamique. Ils ont documenté la nouvelle conception de l'espace par la confrontation de l'intérieur et de l'extérieur.

Le geste pour nous ne sera plus un moment fixé du dynamisme universel: il sera décidément la sensation dynamique éternisée comme telle. **BOCCIONI.**

EXPRESSIONISME

C'est du cubisme et du futurisme que fût fabriqué le hachis, le mystique beefsteak allemand: l'expressionisme.

CUBISM

What distinguishes cubism from precedent painture is this: not to be an art of imitation but a conception that tends to rise itself as creation. **APOLLINAIRE.**

Instead of the impressionist illusion of space based on the perspective of air and the naturalism of colour, cubism offers the simpel and abstracted forms in their precise relations of character and measure. **ALLARD.**

FUTURISM

Futurists have abolished quietness and statism and have demonstrated movement, dynamism. They have documentated the new conception of space by confrontation of interior and exterior.

For us gesture will not any more be a fixed moment of universal dynamism: it will decidedly be the dynamic sensation eternalised as such. **BOCCIONI.**

EXPRESSIONISM

From cubism and futurism has been chopped the minced meat, the mystic german beefsteak: expressionism.

PROUN

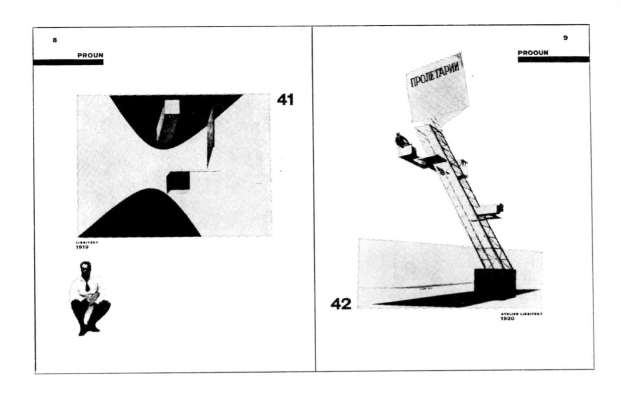

41

LISSITZKY
1919

9

PROOUN

ПРОЛЕТАРИИ

42

ATELIER LISSITZKY
1920

NEO-PLASTIZISMUS

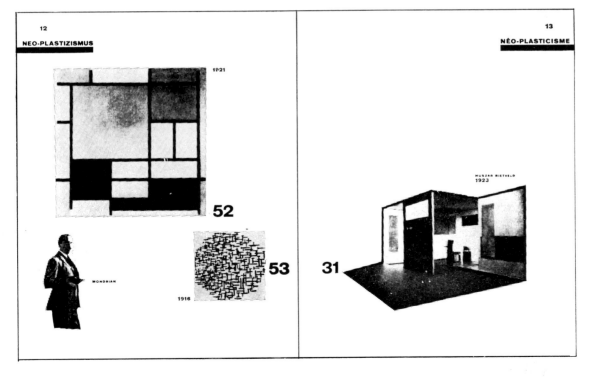

1921

52

MONDRIAN

53

1916

13

NÉO-PLASTICISME

HUSZAR RIETVELD
1923

31

El Lissitsky.
Left: Pages from *The isms of art*, 1925.
Below: Advertisement for carbon paper,
1924.

El Lissitzky, 1924.
Poster design for Pelikan ink.
Photogram.

Theo van Doesburg, 1921.
These visual poems, below and on pages
88 and 89, appeared in a special number
of *de Stijl* entitled *Anthologie-Bonset*.
I. K. Bonset was one of the pseudonyms
adopted by van Doesburg.

DE STIJL

**MAANDBLAD VOOR NIEUWE KUNST, WETENSCHAP
EN KULTUUR. REDACTIE: THEO VAN DOESBURG.
ABONNEMENT BINNENLAND F 6.-, BUITENLAND F 7.50
PER JAARGANG. ADRES VAN REDACTIE EN ADMINISTR.
HAARLEMMERSTRAAT 73A LEIDEN (HOLLAND).**

4e JAARGANG No. 11.   **NOVEMBER 1921.**

LETTERKLANKBEELDEN (1921)

IV (in dissonanten)

```
U¹  J—      m¹  n¹
U   J—      m¹  n¹
V—  F—      K¹  Q¹
F¹  V—      Q¹  K¹
X¹  Q¹      V¹  W¹
X¹  Q¹      W   V
U¹  J—      m—  n—
        g¹
A—  O—      P¹  B¹
A—  O—      P¹  B¹
D—  T—      O¹  E¹
d   t       o   e
        O¹ E¹
        B¹ D¹
Z¹ C  S    B  P  D
        j
```

Aanteekening: te lezen van links naar rechts. Voor de teekens zie men Stijl no. 7.

X-Beelden (1920)

hé hé hé
hebt gij 't lichaamlijk ervaren
hebt gij 't lichaamlijk ervaren
hebt gij 't li **CHAAM** lijk er **VA** ren

O^n

— ruimte en
— tijd
verleden heden toekomst
het achterhierenginds
het doorelkaâr van 't niet en de verschijning

     kleine verfrommelde almanak
     die men ondersteboven leest

MIJN KLOK STAAT STIL

     uitgekauwd sigaretteeindje op 't
ZIG - ZAG   **WITTE SERVET**

vochtig bruin
ontbinding
GEEST
346   **VRACHT AU TO MO BIEL**

DWARS   trillend   onvruchtbaar   middelpunt

caricatuur der zwaarte
uomo electrico

     rose en grauw en diep wijnrood
de scherven van de kosmos vind ik in m'n thee

Aanteekening: O^n: te lezen nul^n; — ruimte en — tijd: te lezen min ruimte en min tijd.

Christian E. M. Küpper was born in Utrecht in August 1883 and early in life assumed the name of Theo van Doesburg. At the age of 16 he began to study painting and he had his first exhibition, in The Hague, in 1908. In 1912 he was art critic of the progressive newspaper *Eenheid*. Two years later he was conscripted and served in the army until 1916.

In 1917 van Doesburg, together with the painters van der Leck, Mondrian, and Huszar, the writer Kok, and the architect Oud, founded the group they named de Stijl and in August of that year they published the first number of their journal. By August 1918, when they issued their manifesto, the original members of the group had been joined by the sculptor Vantongerloo, and the architects, Wils and van't Hoff.

By 1920 van Doesburg's activities had expanded beyond writing and painting into architecture and sculpture, and under the pseudonyms of I. K. Bonset and Aldo Carmini he was also publishing Dadaist poems.

From 1921 until 1923 van Doesburg lived in Weimar where he conducted a course of lectures on de Stijl that were mainly attended by Bauhaus pupils.

In 1922 van Doesburg published, in Holland, under the name of I. K. Bonset, the first of four numbers of *Mécano*, a journal that was Dadaist both in content and in style of presentation. In September he organized the Weimar congress which was attended by both Constructivists and Dadaists, including Tzara, Schwitters, Arp, Richter, Lissitzky, and Moholy-Nagy.

Between 1920 and 1924 the influence of de Stijl had spread throughout Europe. De Stijl designs were exhibited by the Paris art dealer Léonce Rosenberg in 1923, and the following year van Doesburg lectured in Prague and Vienna. Rietveld completed his celebrated Utrecht house in 1924, and in the following year Oud designed the Café de Unie in Rotterdam.

The basis of de Stijl work, whether in architecture, sculpture, furniture, painting or typography, was the rectangle and the use of black, white, and grey and the primary colours, red, blue, and yellow. But about 1924 van Doesburg, who had by then moved to Paris, began to work on a number of paintings and *contra compositions* in which he arranged his rectangles obliquely. He considered that the oblique created a more

(Uit de serie: SOLDATEN 1916)

RUITER

Stap

Paard

STAP

PAARD

Stap

Paard.

STAPPE   PAARD

STAPPE   PAARD

STAPPE   PAARD

STAPPE PAARD   STAPPE PAARD

STEPPE PAARD   STEPPE PAARD

STEPPE PAARD   STEPPE PAARD

STIPPE PAARD STIPPE PAARD STIPPE PAARD

STIP   PAARD

STIP   PAARD

STIP

WOLK

VOORBIJTREKKENDE TROEP

Ran   sel

Ran   sel

Ran   sel

Ran - sel

Ran - sel

Ran - sel

Ran - sel

Ran - sel

BLik - ken - tr**o**mmel

BLik - ken - tr**o**mmel

BLikken TRommel

RANSEL

BLikken trommel

BLikken trommel

BLikken trommel

RANSEL

Blikken trommel
Blikken trommel
Blikken trommel
RANSEL
BLikken trommel
Blikken trommel
Ransel
Blikken trommel
Ransel
Blikken trommel
RAN

Rui schen
Rui   schen
Rui   schen
Rui   schen
Ruischen
Ruisch . . .
Rui . . .
Ru . . .
Ru . . .
R . . .
R . . .
r . .

DE TROM

Rrrrr <u>om</u>

Rrrrr <u>om</u>

Rrrrr - om
DE trom
De drom
De trom
Rrrr - om
BOM

(zeer snel)

Bij den dom
Met den trom
Bij den zwarten dom
Met den hollen trom
<u>Rrrr - om</u>

Marcheeren!
Geweren!
DE zwarte soldaten!
De schuine geweren!
Rrr - om
<u>BOM.</u>

Title lettering by Theo van Doesburg, 1917.

dynamic effect and it led him to formulate the theory of Elementarism which he later published as a manifesto. Mondrian, however, was strongly opposed to this innovation which he saw as a departure from the fundamental principles of de Stijl. He considered that the oblique expressed 'eternal movement' and destroyed the 'cosmic equilibrium' and harmony which he regarded as the essential objectives of de Stijl work, and he forecast that this 'superficial attempt to find a new plastic expression' would lead to a 'return to nature'.

In 1925 van Doesburg's *Grundbegriffe der neuen gestaltenden Kunst* was issued as Volume 6 in the series of Bauhaus books published under the editorship of Gropius and Moholy-Nagy.

In 1927 van Doesburg designed the interior of *L'Aubette*, a café-restaurant in Strasbourg, and he published the results of this commission in his magazine, *de Stijl*, in 1928. In 1930 he prepared plans for his own house at Meudon-Val Fleury, but this building, which was also to provide a collective studio for the de Stijl group, was unfinished when he died at Davos, at the age of 47, on 7 March 1931.

Theo van Doesburg, 1922.
The cover design, actual size, of the third issue of *Mécano*. This publication consisted of a single sheet, size $12\frac{3}{4} \times 20$ inches, printed on both sides, in black ink on red paper, and folded to $6\frac{3}{8} \times 5$ inches.

Inhalt: DADA IN HOLLAND. KOK: GEDICHT. BONSET: GEDICHT; AAN ANNA BLOEME.
PICABIA: ZEICHNUNG. HANNAH HÖCH: ZEICHNUNG; WEISSLACKIERTE TÜTE

MERZ
1
HOLLAND
DADA

DA
DA · DA
DA

JANUAR 1923
HERAUSGEBER: KURT SCHWITTERS
HANNOVER · WALDHAUSENSTRASSE 5ᴵᴵ

Kurt Schwitters, 1923.
Cover of the first issue of *Merz*.
Slightly reduced.
The original is printed in black
on grey paper.

Kurt Schwitters was born at Hanover in June 1887. His studies at the Academy of Dresden were followed by two terms at the Berlin Academy and in 1915 he married Helma Fischer. A brief period of military service in 1917, spent in a regimental office in Hanover – 'I'm fighting on every front of our parade ground', he said – was followed by two terms as an architectural student at the Hanover technical college.

In 1919 he produced his first MERZ pictures composed of 'disparate elements merged into a work of art with the help of nails and glue, paper and rags, hammers and oil,

Memoiren Anna Blumes in Bleie,
Freiburg, 1922.
Presentation copy with montage by Kurt Schwitters.

2

PYJAMA

Was ist DADA in der LUFT?

GROOTE BALANS OPRUIMING
KOPF KÜHL, FÜSSE WARM

»Que fait DADA? 50 francs de récompense a celui qui trouve le moyen de nous expliquer DADA.« »Es bildet ein Talent sich in der Stille, sich ein Charakter in dem Strom der Welt.« »De Professor Janßen had de gewoonte, om altijd in zijn linnen jas te loopen, niet alleen in de college tijden, maar ook buiten. Op die manier gekleed liep hij eens voor zijn woning, op iemand te wachten. Daar trad en vreemde op hem toe en vroeg hem: »Wat is dada?« »DADA est un puits sur l'amour.«

3

GROOTE KOE

DADA ISMUS IN HOLLAND

DADA

in Holland ist ein Novum. Nur ein Holländer, I. K. BONSET, ist Dadaist. (Er wohnt in Wien.) Und eine Holländerin, PETRO VAN DOESBURG, ist Dadaistin. (Sie wohnt in Weimar.) Ich kenne dann noch einen holländischen Pseudodadaisten, er ist aber kein Dadaist. Holland aber,

HOLLAND IST DADA

Unser Erscheinen in Holland glich einem gewaltigen Siegeszug. Ganz Holland ist jetzt dada, weil es immer schon dada war.

Unser Publikum fühlt, daß es DADA ist und glaubt, dada kreischen, dada schreien, dada lispeln, dada singen, dada heulen, dada schelten zu müssen. Kaum hat jemand von uns, die wir in Holland Träger der dadaistischen Bewegung sind, das Podium betreten, so erwachen im Publikum die verschlafenen dadaistischen Instinkte, und es empfängt uns ein dadaistisches Heulen und Zähneklappen. Aber wir sind die dadaistische Hauskapelle, wir werden Ihnen eins blasen.

64 NEU ➤ Jedermann seine eigene Redaktion. ◀ NEU

DAS MERZBILD. K. SCHWITTERS.

SAMMLUNG STADTMUSEUM DRESDEN.

Lanke trr gll
P P P P P
oka oka oka oka
Lanke trr gll
pi pi pi pi
züka züka züka züka
Lanke trr gll
rmp
rnf
Lanke trr gll
rmp
P P P P P
rnf
pi pi pi pi
Lanke trr gll
P P P P P
zi U J u
zi U Au
zi U J u
zi U A   K. Schwitters

GOLDACKERSPRÜCHE.
Die Folge von Deutschlands wirtschaftlich und politisch schwieriger
Lage wird sein der vorangegangene verlustreiche Krieg.

G, Zeitschrift für elementare Gestaltung. Sturm. Manomètre.
Stijl. Mecano. Ma.

Besser ist schlechter als gut. Karl Minder.

Merz 1: Hollanddada.
Merz 2: i
Merz 4: Banalitäten.
Merz 3: 6 Lithos von
K. Schwitters.

Das ist ARPlid mein Land.
homo homini dada

H. Hoech.
Dr. Döhmann.

MERZ 5 ist eine Mappe von 7 Arpaden von
Hans Arp. Preis 10 Dollar oder gleicher
Wert anderer Währung. Es sind folgende:
1. Litho: Schnurrhut.
2. Litho: Das Meer.
3. Litho: Ein Nabel.
4. Litho: Die Nabelflasche.
5. Litho: Schnurruhr.
6. Litho: Eierschläger.
7. Litho: Arabische Acht.
Zu beziehen vom Merzverlag.

ARABISCHE SPRICHWÖRTER.
Die linke Hand der rächenden Nemesis ist die
rechte Hand jener Philadelphia, von welcher Schiller be-
hauptet, daß sie Seelen fordert. ■ Braut schau wem?
Ein trockener Hund pißt gern auf Lösdpapier. Ein aus-
gestopfter Hund wirft gern auf Lösdpapier keinen Schatten. Ein aus-
ein angelsächsischer Genitiv.
HANS ARP

56

DIE GUTE REKLAME IST BILLIG.

Ein geringes Maß hochwertiger Reklame, die in jeder Weise Qualität verrät, übersteigt an Wirkung eine vielfache Menge ungeeigneter, ungeschickt organisierter Reklame.
Max Burchartz.

MERZ

11

RED. MERZ, HANNOVER, WALDHAUSENSTR. 5 II.

TYPO
REKLAME

EINIGE THESEN ZUR GESTALTUNG DER REKLAME VON MAX BURCHARTZ:

Die Reklame ist die Handschrift des Unternehmers. Wie die Handschrift ihren Urheber, so verrät die Reklame Art, Kraft und Fähigkeit einer Unternehmung. Das Maß der Leistungsfähigkeit, Qualitätspflege, Solidität, Energie und Großzügigkeit eines Unternehmens spiegelt sich in Sachlichkeit, Klarheit, Form und Umfang seiner Reklame. Hochwertige Qualität der Ware ist erste Bedingung des Erfolges. Die zweite: Geeignete Absatzorganisation; deren unentbehrlicher Faktor ist gute Reklame. Die gute Reklame verwendet moderne Mittel. Wer reist heute in einer Kutsche? Gute Reklame bedient sich neuester zeitgemäßer Erfindungen als neuer Werkzeuge der Mitteilung. Wesentlich ist die Neuartigkeit der Formengebung. Abgeleierte banale Formen der Sprache und künstlerischen Gestaltung müssen vermieden werden.   Zitiert aus Gestaltung der Reklame, Bochum, Bongardstrasse 15.

K. SCHWITTERS.
Signetentwurf für Adolf
Rothenberg

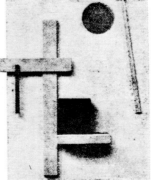

DIE GUTE REKLAME
ist sachlich, ist klar und knapp, verwendet moderne Mittel, hat Schlagkraft der Form, ist billig.
MAX BURCHARTZ.

WERBEN SIE BITTE FÜR MERZ. *Pelikan*-Nummer.

Merzrelief von Kurt Schwitters siehe Seite 91

SIGNETENTWURF FÜR DAS WORT PELIKAN VON KURT SCHWITTERS

4001 Beste Buch- und Schreibtinte. Eisengallustinte, fließt bläulich, wird tiefschwarz. Liefert Schrift von unbegrenzter Dauer. Angenehm leichtflüssig.
5001 Buch- und Kopiertinte. Eisengallustinte, fließt bläulich, wird schwarz. Liefert auf der Kopierpresse 2 bis 3 Kopien. Kann auch in Büchern verwandt werden, ohne darin abzuklatschen.
3001 Starke Kopiertinte. Echte Blauholztinte, fließt violett-schwarz. Schrift und Kopien dunkeln schwarz nach. Gibt auf der Kopiermaschine 3 bis 6 Kopien. Auch nach längerer Zeit noch kopierfähig. Nicht für Bücher bestimmt.

3001   4001   5001

NASCI NASCI NASCI NASCI LISSITZKY
NASCI NASCI NASCI NASCI SCHWITTERS

NASCI

Wenn Sie Ihre inneren Beschwerden auf vollständig ungefährliche Weise aufbürsten wollen, wenn Sie, ohne die Plattform zu besteigen, hineinsehen wollen in die gegenüberliegende Kellerwohnung, wenn Sie Blumen säen und dafür Samen ernten wollen, wenn Sie ohne zu wollen weder können noch wollen müssen, wenn Sie im Namen der vorderen drei Ecken eines ausgewachsenen Hundes das Quadrat quadrieren wollen, wenn Sie überhaupt für Ihre Seele und speciell Ihre Bildung tun und lassen wollen, was unsere Zeit braucht, wenn Sie sich und mich überzeugen wollen von der Kraft unserer Kunst, heutigen Tages zu ebener Erde, so lesen Sie regelmäßig die Zeitschrift MERZ Bestellen Sie sofort ein Abonnement für 3 Mark oder 2 Fl. oder 5 Schweizer Franken oder 1 Dollar bei der Redaktion **Merz, Hannover, Waldhausenstr. 5, II.** ████████ **Bestellen Sie gleich.**

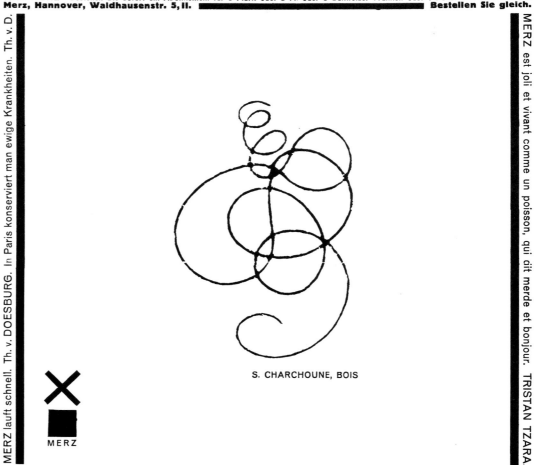

S. CHARCHOUNE, BOIS

MERZ

MERZ lauft schnell. Th. v. DOESBURG. In Paris konserviert man ewige Krankheiten. Th. v. D.

MERZ est joli et vivant comme un poisson, qui dit merde et bonjour. TRISTAN TZARA.

EINGESANDTE ZEITSCHRIFTEN: BROOM, New York; CONTIMPORANUL, Bucarest; DISK, Prag; DER EINZIGE, Berlin-Friedenau; FRÜHLICHT, Magdeburg; G, Berlin; THE LITTLE REVIEW, New York; LUCIFER, Lyon; MA, Wien; MANOMÈTRE, Lyon; MECANO, Leiden; NEUE KULTUR-KORRESPONDENZ, Berlin; NOI, Rom; HET OVERZICHT, Anvers; PROVERBE, Paris; THE S. 4. N. MAGAZINE, Northampton; SEPT ARTS, Bruxelles; DE STIJL, Leiden; DER STURM, Berlin; LA VIE DES LETTRES, Neuilly-Paris; ZENIT, Belgrad; DIE ZONE, Brünn; DER ZWEEMANN, Hannover; ZWROTNICA, Krakau.

NASCI NASCI NASCI NASCI SCHWITTERS
NASCI NASCI NASCI NASCI LISSITZKY

NASCI

VORANZEIGE. Das nächste Heft, MERZ 8 und 9, wird eine Doppelnummer unter dem Titel NASCI. NASCI ist von Lissitzky und Schwitters sehr sorgfältig zusammengestellt. Zu diesem und dem nächsten Heft verdanke ich einige Klischees folgenden Verlägen: De Stijl, Leiden; Ernst Wasmuth, Berlin, Markgrafenstr. 5; Wasmuths Monatshefte; Gustav Fischer Verlag, Jena; Frühlichtverlag, Magdeburg; Karl Peters; Querschnittverlag, Frankfurt a. M.; Bauhausverlag, München, Maximilianstr. 18.

Kurt Schwitters:
design for a single-alphabet phonetic
type, 1927, right.

MŪSJK JM Lēben dēR VÖLKeR AM 2.JŪLJ
20 ŪhR dJRJGJeRT JM OPeRNhAUS
WARSₜhAUS beRŪhMTeR dJRJGeNT WeRKe
POLNJSₜheR MeJSTeR PReJSe 1–5Mk.

Back cover of *Merz* 7, published in
January 1924. The original is printed in
black on light blue paper.
(From the seventh issue, the page size of
Merz was greatly increased.)

paint, parts of machinery and bits of lace'. In Germany, reproductions of his work and
his poem 'Anna Blume' were published in *Der Sturm*, and, in Zurich, the Dadaist
Tristan Tzara published two of Schwitter's poems and reproduced one of his MERZ
compositions in his magazine *Der Zeltweg*. In 1921, Schwitters went on a lecture tour
to Prague with Raoul Hausmann and Hannah Höch, and later with van Doesburg he
campaigned for Dada in Holland. In Germany, at this time, Schwitters had frequent
meetings with Lissitzky and during the visit to Holland he became, through van
Doesburg, closely acquainted with many members of de Stijl. From 1921 the
influence of Constructivism is clearly apparent in his work. He contributed to van
Doesburg's magazine *Mécano*, and in the autum of 1922 he took an active part in the
meeting of Constructivists and Dadaists in Weimar. In January of the following year
he published the first issue of *Merz*, and during the course of 1923 a further five
numbers appeared with contributions from Arp, Mondrian, Lissitzky, Man Ray,
Picabia, Tzara, and many others. A double-number (8/9, *Merz-Nasci*) published the
following spring was edited jointly by Schwitters and Lissitzky, and *Merz* 11 was
devoted to the subject of typography in advertising. 'Periodicals sprouted like
mushrooms in those days', Sophie Lissitzky has written, 'and like mushrooms they
often had only a short existence.' But *Merz* was an exception, and between 1923 and
1932 when the final issue appeared, Schwitters published twenty-four numbers. In
1927 Schwitters, together with Baumeister, Tschichold, Vordemberge-Gildewart and
others, formed the Ring neuer Werbegestalter (circle of new advertising designers)
and in 1928 he published in *Der Sturm* an article on creative typography.

He worked as a typographer on the 1929 Dammerstock exhibition in Karlsruhe, under
Gropius, and he was for several years typographical adviser to the City of Hanover.
During the early 1930's, as the political situation in Germany worsened, he spent an
increasing amount of time in Norway, and in January 1937 he left Germany for the last
time and settled near Oslo. In June 1940, following the German invasion of Norway,
he escaped across the North Sea to Scotland. In 1945 he settled in Westmorland,
where he died at Ambleside, in January 1948.

H. N. Werkman.
Front page of the first issue of *The next call*, published in 1923.

Hendrik Nicolaas Werkman was an artist who made his livelihood as a printer and who used the materials and equipment available in a printing office to create many of his most interesting pictures.

Werkman was born in April 1882 at Leens, in the province of Groningen, where both his father and grandfather were veterinary surgeons. In 1891, when he was nine years old, his grandfather died and his father too within three months, leaving his mother almost penniless. The veterinary practice was taken over by his uncle, Hendrik Garmt, and two years later, in 1893, Werkman's mother and her three sons, of whom Hendrik was the middle one, moved first to Assen and the following year to the city of Groningen, where Werkman was to live for the rest of his life.

Werkman's printing workshop in Groningen, c.1908.

The first indication of his interest in art revealed itself soon after a visit to the Van Gogh exhibition in Groningen in 1896, when he was fourteen (His admiration for Van Gogh was to manifest itself many years later when he named the child of his second marriage, Vincent). Some three years later he became interested in photography and in the following year, 1900, after a disappointing performance at school, he was apprenticed to Borgesius, a firm of printers in Sappemeer. For the next three years he worked in various printing houses, becoming increasingly interested in newspapers, and in 1903 he was employed as a journalist on the *Groningen Dagblad*, and later on the *Nieuwe Groninger Courant*.

When, in 1907, he became engaged to Jansje Cremer he resigned from the newspaper and took a job as a foreman at Knoop, a firm of printers in Wildervank. However, within twelve months he had decided to start his own press, at 5 Peperstraat in Groningen. He married Jansje Cremer two years later, in 1909, and with financial help from her family he was able to expand the business, first employing a boy of twelve, Wybren Bos, who was to remain a faithful assistant throughout Werkman's life, and eventually increasing his staff to thirty. In 1912 he built new premises for the firm in Pelerstraat.

In 1917 his wife died and when, in the following year, he decide to marry Pieternella Supheert, the Cremer family withdrew their financial support. The result of this was that the firm began to founder and in 1923 Werkman was forced to sell out, retaining only two of his employees, one of whom was Bos. He then opened a new printing shop, on a very small scale, in the attic of a canal-side warehouse on the Lage der A. This period was, however, a turning-point in his life, as the lack of work enabled him to devote time to producing prints and painting. In a letter to F. R. A. Henkels, many years later (12 May 1941) Werkman wrote:

'Looking at it from a conventional point of view, I declined as rapidly in a couple of years as I had progressed in ten. But like a wet poodle I shook off everything which was hindering me and then stood for a while almost alone. Frankly, sometimes I didn't even understand myself. But I always thought, ''What you lose now is really something won''. I never mourned seeming losses. But the situation was dismal indeed; no wonder that the first prints which I made at that time were dark and gloomy . . .'

Front page of *The next call* numbers 2 and 5 published in 1923 and 1924. The original of No.2 is in yellow and black, No.5 is in orange and dark blue.

He had started to paint about the same time as his first wife's death, and he also made etchings and lithographs. In 1920 he had joined the Groningen society of artists called De Ploeg with whom he frequently exhibited. He became more deeply interested in art and, from 1921 to 1922, he published an art journal *Blad voor kunst* concerned mainly with the work of Groningen artists, but also sometimes reflecting Werkman's emerging interests, for example his review of the poem 'Bezette Stad' by the Flemish poet, Paul van Ostayen.

He was becoming aware, at this time, of the international *avant-garde* movement, having seen the de Stijl exhibition in Groningen, in 1922, and, probably, the exhibition of Russian art and German Expressionism, shown in Amsterdam shortly afterwards. Werkman seems to have become increasingly disappointed with the conservative attitude of many members of De Ploeg and in 1923 he decide to produce a new publication under the English title *The next call* of which nine issues were to appear between then and 1926. Werkman wrote many of the texts himself, although his name did not appear, and he amusingly credited the publication to 'Travailleur et cie' (a joke which van Doesburg – who criticised Werkman for not acknowledging individual contributors – seems not to have understood).

The first issue contained, on its front page, an image produced directly from part of a lock, printed in red (and this was also used on the envelope), and the same shape occurs again in issues two, three and five. In many issues Werkman made use of his highly original technique, placing the paper on the bed of the handpress and the inked type or other material face down upon it. In this way Werkman was able to combine into a single stage the creative and the printing process. The method enabled him to vary each element of a print (colour, inking, pressure, etc.) until he had achieved precisely the effect he required. Two or more shapes could be printed simultaneously in different colours, and each of the resulting prints was in fact unique, in a way that would not be achieved by conventional printing. The use of this method explains why one may discover discrepancies between different reproductions of the same edition of a Werkman publication.

With the publication of *The next call* he moved away from painting and began to experiment increasingly with the materials he found everywhere around him in his workshop.

'Printing', he said, 'offers more possibilities than painting. It enables me to express myself more freely, and also more directly.' It was the moment when, as Jan Martinet has written in his book *The next call*, Werkman exchanged his Sunday-painter status for that of a professional artist, a notion echoed by Werkman himself in *The next call*, number six, when he wrote 'he has his Sundays, six days a week, except on Sunday'.

Werkman received avant-garde magazines such as Cernik's *La zone* from Czechoslovakia and Lioubimir Mitsitch's *Zenith* from Belgrade, in exchange for further correspondence from any of the artists of the major movements. He is known to have sent *The next call* to Peeters and Seufor, then in Antwerp, and the Blok Group in Poland.

At the same time as he produced the first issue of *The next call*, Werkman began to produce experimental prints to which he gave the names 'druksels' and 'tiksels'. These names, which derive from *drukken*, meaning 'to print', and *tikken*, a slang term for 'to type', emphasize the experimental nature of the prints.

His earliest known druksels are two prints entitled 'chimneys' (*schoornstenen*) produced in 1923 which reflect, in their dark colours, his personal and business

H. N. Werkman, 1924.
From *The next call* 4, published in an
edition of approximately forty copies on
the occasion of Lenin's death.

LENIN

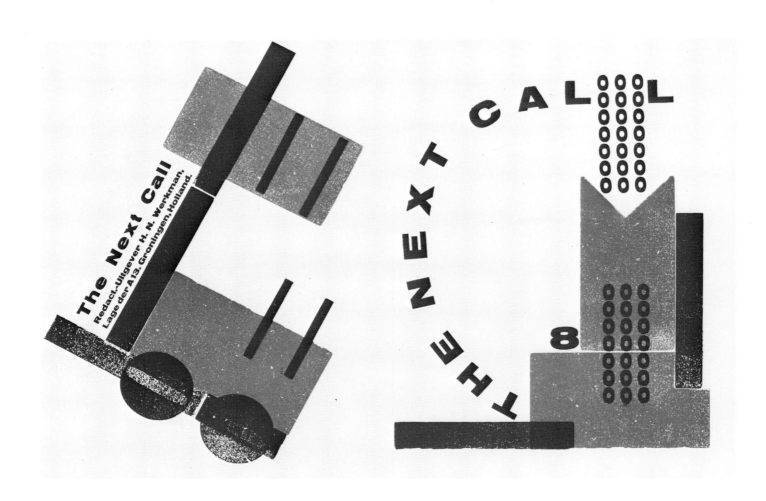

H. N. Werkman.
Left: Pages from *The next call* 8 1926.
The originals are in dark red and black.
Right: Drucksel: *The cylinder press,*
1925.

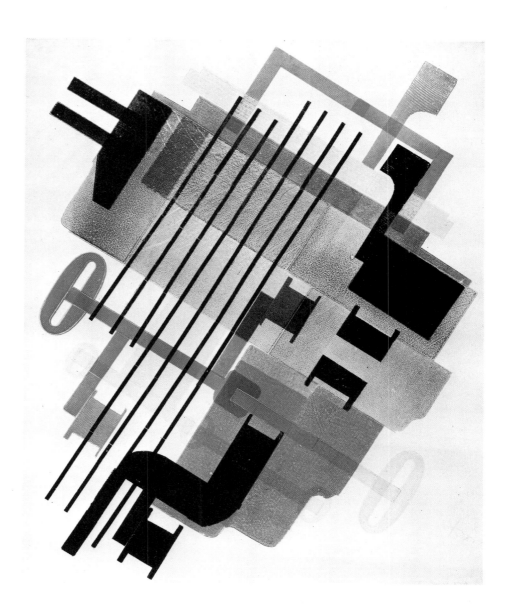

This print, left, entitled *Composition with the letter O* was produced by Werkman in 1927. The original is in black, red, dark blue and yellow.

H.N. Werkman, 1926.
Front page of *The next call* 9.
The ninth and final issue was produced in a larger format than the earlier issues. The size of the original is 350 × 215 mm (13$\frac{7}{8}$ × 8$\frac{3}{4}$ inches) and is printed in red, black and dark blue on cream laid paper.

problems at that time. Gradually, however, his prints became brighter in colour as can be seen in his compositions of some three or four years later.

Because Werkman was short of money he bought his inks in small quantities and worked at any one time with a limited number of colours. When he bought a new supply of ink he often changed the colours so that, to some extent, his prints can be dated by the colour he used. Many of his prints of the 1920's are abstract in concept, and though some contain recognizable letters and numbers, others introduce shapes and forms that cannot be readily associated with type.

Werkman not only used the type, wood letters and other printing materials that came readily to hand, but pressed into use anything from which an image could be obtained. He frequently used the backs of wood letters and he sometimes cut cardboard to form the shapes he desired. He also sometimes changed the shape of a rectangular block of wood by laying a strip of paper between it and the sheet of paper to be printed so that the part covered by the strip remained blank after printing. Werkman wrote about his technique in a letter to F. R. A. Henkels:

'I use an old handpress for my prints; so the impression is done vertically, and the pressure can be regulated instinctively. Sometimes you have to press hard, sometimes very lightly, sometimes one half of the block is heavily inked, the other half sparsely, also by printing the first layer of paint on a piece of paper you get a paler shade which is used for the definitive print, and at other times I press the first impression onto the definitive version again . . . No one works in this way, I don't think anyone could get the same colour effects without a lot of practice and experience. Sometimes a single print goes under the press up to fifty times.'

He extended his technique by using the 'stamp' method for small typographic forms such as rules, commas, individual letters or pointing fists which he simply inked and pressed onto the paper.

Werkman's typographic works are distinguished not only by his highly individual printing technique but also by his sensitivity to the subtle and sometimes accidental effect that typographic material can yield. He exploited the textures of the wood letters themselves, deliberately bringing out the qualities in the grain of wood letters and enjoying the scratches and other blemishes in old type for the individuality these gave to the letter. In the same way he took great care in the choice of ink and paper and two of Werkman's comments underline his love for the materials he was handling: 'some paper is so beautiful that you would like just to caress it and leave it chaste' and 'ink is an even more delicate creature'.

Werkman's output, in view of his technique, was necessarily small and the editions of his works extremely limited, seldom more than forty copies.

So far as is known, all Werkman's tiksels were made between 1923 and 1929, and all are in black on white. Many of these contain recognizable images and, like the druksels, they echo the work of the Dadaists: the druksels being akin to some Dada collages, while the tiksels reflect Guillaume Apollinaire's 'Ideogrammes lyriques' and Paul van Ostaijen's 'Bezette Stad'.

The term 'Hot Printing' has in recent years been used to describe much of Werkman's output and was adopted as the title of the major catalogue of his work produced by the H. N. Werkman Foundation in 1963. Strictly, however, 'Hot Printing' is not the description of a technique but the title of a series of druksels made between 1924 and 1928, of which nineteen survive, although there may originally have been more. These sheets were issued by Werkman either singly or in combination, accompanied by one or more of his own poems and contained in a cover with the title 'Hot Printing'. The same covers were used for different texts and prints. Some of the poems were reproduced again later in his *Pesach 1936*. 'Hot Printing' which so aptly describes his technique stems, of course, from the term 'Hot Jazz'.

During the 1920's Werkman's financial situation continued to deteriorate and in 1927 he found himself left with only a single assistant, Bos, and a new cylinder press which his friends had helped him to buy.

At this time he produced relatively little, but once his problems had begun to subside he produced more work and he contacted Michel Seuphor who was now in Paris and who wanted to arrange an exhibition for him there. Seuphor wrote to Werkman on 30 May 1927:

'You are not known in Paris, but you have no right to remain so indefinitely because your work greatly merits the appreciation of a public larger than that in Groningen ... we ask nothing better than to organize an exhibition for you in Paris.'

H. N. Werkman.
Announcement of a meeting, 1926.

woensdag 17
november 8¹₂
uur 's avonds
in prinsenhof

vergadering

de ploeg

Notulen.
Ingekomen stukken
Verkiezing bestuurslid
    " lid kouterred.
Abonnement tijdschrift
Bespr. tentoonst. A'dam
Uitg. van een grafisch
Ploegboek, met prijsvr.
voor een omslag
Mededeelingen
Rondvraag

met het oog op de
belangrijke punten
der agenda is op-
komst van alle le-
den noodzakelijk.

de ploeg
18 t entoonstelling
/2 eekeningen

H. N. Werkman.
Exhibition announcement, 1928.

In August 1929 Werkman went to Cologne and Paris with his friend, the Dutch Expressionist Jan Wiegers. While in Paris he tried to contact Michel Seuphor, but without success. However, his visit to Paris stimulated him to make a series of prints, incorporating as formal elements the steps, halls and arches of the Metro. A year later, through Michel Seuphor's efforts, Werkman was invited to exhibit two prints with the group 'Cercle et Carré'.

Werkman's second marriage was finally dissolved in June 1930, and a few months later his mother died. The following summer he moved to 30 Princesseweg with one of his sons, but this was for Werkman clearly a period of emotional instability – he twice considered and then abandoned the idea of remarrying during 1931 – and he entertained the idea of emigrating to Tahiti. In 1934 he met Greet van Leeuwen whom he married two years later.

A poster which he produced for the Groningen gasworks exhibition in the Summer of 1934 employed a new technique. In 1929, he had begun to apply the ink roller direct onto the paper and, now, in 1934 he extended this method by using paper shapes as stencils. At this time, too, his work became more figurative. Indeed, one may say of many of his works from that time onwards, that he was using the press and printing ink to create paintings rather than prints in the sense that is normally understood by that description.

In the late 1930's, Willem Sandberg, who had been appointed curator at the Stedelijk

H. N. Werkman, 1933
Poster for performance of Elmer L. Rice's
The adding machine. Original in red and
blue, size 648×505 mm, (25½×20
inches).

Museum, Amsterdam, in succession to van Regteren Altena in 1937, saw some of Werkman's larger prints. Early in 1939 Sandberg was introduced to Werkman in Groningen by Jan Wiegers, and as a result of this meeting Sandberg arranged for Werkman to exhibit at the Helen Spoor Gallery in Amsterdam in November of that year.

With the occupation of Holland in May 1940, Werkman's painting experiments were halted and for several months he confined himself to drawing and painting on cardboard. In November, however, a chance meeting with a group of friends – Adri Buning, August Henkels and Ate Zuithoff – was to result in a new period of intense printing activity which was to continue until the end of his life.

Between 1940 and 1945 Werkman produced a series of forty subversive broadsheets, known as *De blauwe Schuit* (The blue Barge) – a name derived from a painting by Hieronymus Bosch ('The Ship of Fools') and the words of a poem by the sixteenth-century Dutch poet Jacob van Oostvoorne.

H. N. Werkman was arrested by the Nazis and executed with nine others at Bakkeveen on 10 April 1945, three days before the Allied armies reached Northern Holland. Much of his most recent and mature work, which had been seized and taken to the local Gestapo headquarters, was destroyed during the battle of liberation. It is estimated that Werkman produced over 120 oil paintings and more than 600 druksels, but only half of these pictures survived the war.

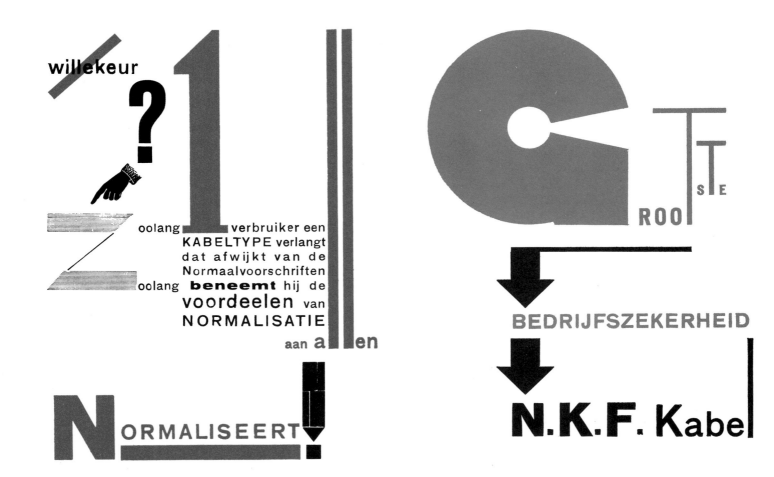

willekeur

?

Zoolang verbruiker een KABELTYPE verlangt dat afwijkt van de Normaalvoorschriften Zoolang **beneemt** hij de voordeelen van NORMALISATIE aan allen

Normaliseert!

GROOTSTE

BEDRIJFSZEKERHEID

N.K.F. Kabel

Pages from a booklet for N K F, slightly reduced, designed by Piet Zwart in 1924. The original of the design on the right is in blue and black.

Piet Zwart's personal mark.

Postcard for LAGA Company, 1923.
Original in red and black.

Piet Zwart was born in May 1885 at Zaandijk, an industrial area north of Amsterdam. From 1902 to 1907 he attended the school of arts and crafts in Amsterdam which was housed in a wing of the Rijksmuseum. This he described, characteristically, as a 'smashing school with no idea of a programme, in which the spare-time teachers did not burden us with their presence – most of the time we were left to develop by ourselves with no interference from above!' In this school there was no division between painting, architecture, and furniture design, and it was here that Zwart began, in his own words, 'to nibble at architecture'. For about five years after leaving the Amsterdam school Zwart taught drawing and history of art at a girls' school in Leeuwarden. It was during this period, in 1911, that he received his first commissions for furniture and interior design. In 1913 he enrolled at the technical college at Delft, but his studies there were brought to an abrupt end by mobilization in 1914.

Piet Zwart made his first contact with de Stijl in 1919 and from then until 1921 he was employed by the architect Jan Wils who was a member of the de Stijl group. Zwart's first exercise in typography was to design a device and letterheading for Wils, which clearly echo the title lettering produced by van Doesburg for his periodical, *de Stijl*, in 1917. In 1921, Zwart left Wils to become assistant to the famous Dutch architect H. P.

JAN WILS
ARCHITECT B.N.A.
VOORBURG

Dm.
Mp.
Bf.
Tp.
Op.

TELEFOON   V 25.   M 2542
POSTCHEQUE EN GIRO 40004

Letterhead for the architect Jan Wils,
designed by Piet Zwart in 1921.

Letterhead for State Experimental
Theatre, 1925. Original in red and black.

VEREENIGING:EXPERIMENTEELTOONEEL

W!JNU

SECRETARIAAT:
ZEESTRAAT 82
TEL. 12292
DEN HAAG
HOLLAND

!

Glazed ceramic letters for First Church of Christ Scientist, The Hague. 1926.

Wrapping paper design by Piet Zwart for Vetpot, 1924. Original in red and green.

Advertisement for N K F,
1924.

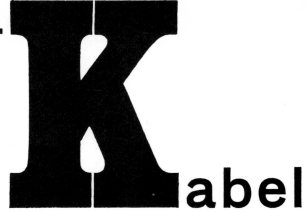

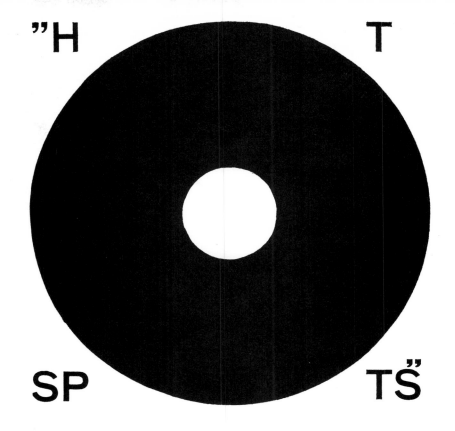

Advertisement for NKF
1926

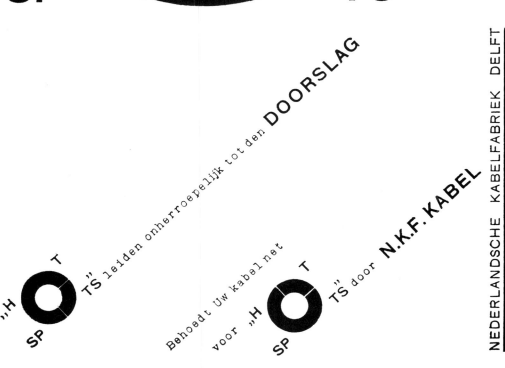

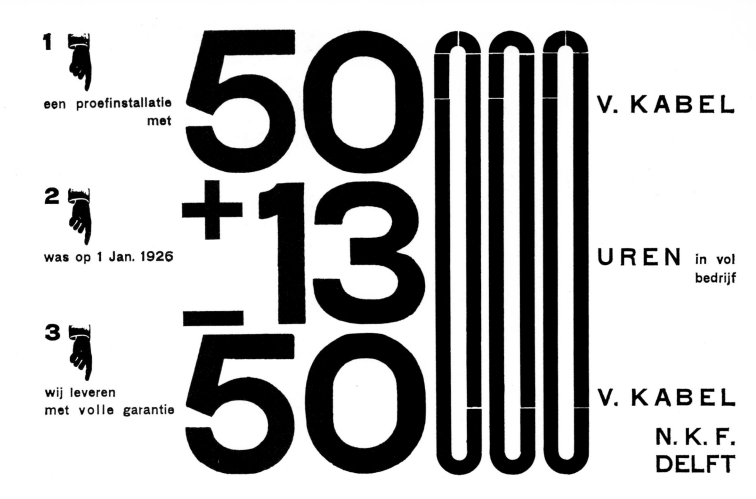

1 → een proefinstallatie met

2 → was op 1 Jan. 1926

3 → wij leveren met volle garantie

50000 +13 -50 V. KABEL UREN in vol bedrijf V. KABEL N.K.F. DELFT

Advertisement for N K F, 1926.

Opposite:
Advertisements for N K F, 1926 and 1928.

Berlage, a post he was to hold for several years. With Berlage he worked on designs for a Christian Science Church (for which he also designed the glazed ceramic title lettering) and a municipal museum, both in The Hague. While working in Berlage's office Zwart produced his first advertisement designs, for a firm of flooring manufacturers in The Hague, and carried out his first commissions for industrial design. About this time too he designed a brochure for Fortoliefabriek in Utrecht. Berlage then introduced Zwart to one of his relatives who was manager of the Nederlandsche Kabelfabriek at Delft and by 1925, at the age of 40, Zwart had begun to devote the greater part of his time to typography. During the next few years he produced many hundreds of designs for advertisements and catalogues for Nederlandsche Kabelfabriek. From 1925 until 1928 he was also architectural correspondent of the daily newspaper *Het Vaderland* published in The Hague. Zwart soon developed a passionate interest in photography. He began to combine photographs (after 1928, his own) and photomontage in his layouts in a strikingly

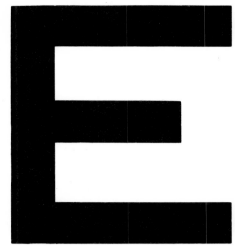
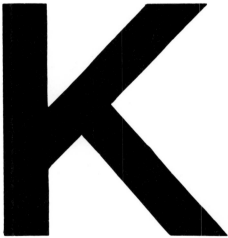

250 10

2 50

10, 25, 50 kv. hoogspanningskabels met papierisolatie.

HOOGSPANNINGSKABELS

N.V. NEDERLANDSCHE KABELFABRIEK DELFT.

lectrolitisch
lectrolitisch
lectrolitisch
lectrolitisch
lectrolitisch
lectrolitisch
lectrolitisch
lectrolitisch
lectrolitisch
lectrolitisch
lectrolitisch
lectrolitisch
lectrolitisch
lectrolitisch
lectrolitisch
lectrolitisch
lectrolitisch
lectrolitisch

operdraad
operdraad
operdraad
operdraad
operdraad
operdraad
operdraad
operdraad
operdraad
operdraad
operdraad
operdraad
operdraad
operdraad
operdraad
operdraad

uit voorraad
uit voorraad
uit voorraad
uit voorraad
uit voorraad
uit voorraad
uit voorraad
uit voorraad
uit voorraad
uit voorraad
uit voorraad
uit uoorraad
uit voorraad
uit voorraad
uit voorraad
uit voorraad

N.V. NEDERLANDSCHE
KABELFABRIEK DELFT
N. K. F

Front and back cover and two double
spreads from catalogue for
Nederlandsche Kabelfabriek, Delft,
designed by Piet Zwart, 1927–8. Greatly
reduced. The original cover design is in
black and yellow.

1927.
1928

2

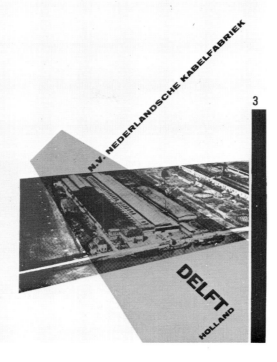

N.V. NEDERLANDSCHE KABELFABRIEK

3

DELFT
HOLLAND

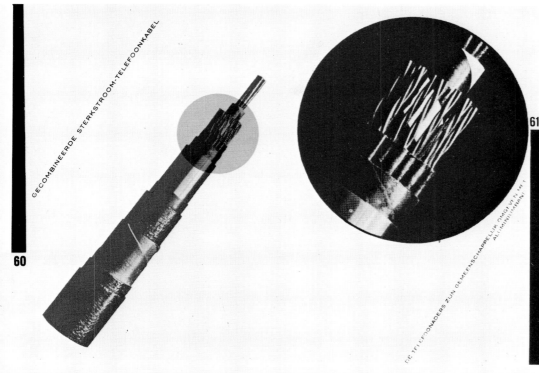

GECOMBINEERDE STERKSTROOM-TELEFOONKABEL

60

61

DE TELEFOONADERS ZIJN GEMEENSCHAPPELIJK OMGEVEN MET
ALUMINIUMBAND

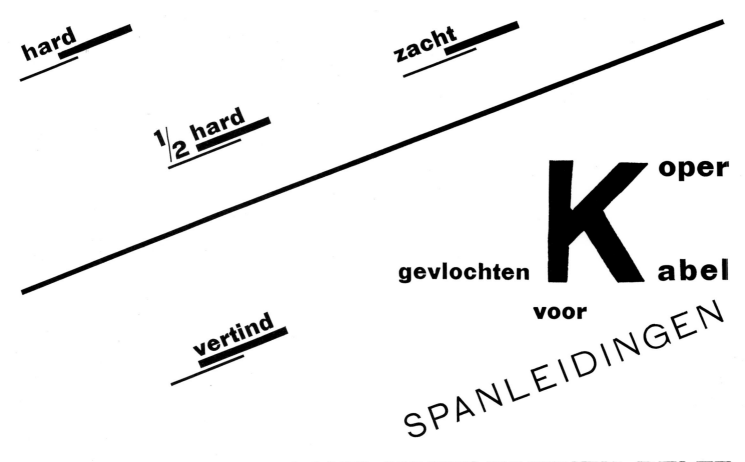

hard

zacht

½ hard

Koper

gevlochten **K**abel

voor

vertind

SPANLEIDINGEN

N.V. NEDERLANDSCHE KABELFABRIEK DELFT

Advertisement for NKF, 1928.

Stamps designed by Piet Zwart, 1931–3

original and highly relevant way. His designs for NKF catalogues and booklets for the Post Office during the late 1920's are full of vigorous and imaginative surprises. His colours continued to be those of de Stijl – primary blue, yellow, and red – but Zwart's clever use of words (he was his own copywriter), his ingenious manipulation of type and rules, his dramatic use of strong-contrast photographs and of negative reproductions, the dexterity with which he superimposed photographs in one strong colour over other photographs in other colours, his use of transparent materials, of cut-out shapes and clever folds, and, indeed, the whole uninhibited pioneering enthusiasm of his attack suddenly charged the printed page with a new power, a new tension, and gave it in effect a new dimension.

In 1929 Zwart designed the first of a series of stamps for the Dutch Post Office which was to mark the beginning of a long association with the PTT. For a short period in 1931 he was a guest-teacher at the Bauhaus. He continued his typographic and photographic activities in Holland throughout the 1930's but shortly before the war (during which he was arrested by the Nazis and held as a hostage) he again turned to industrial design and developed the famous Bruynzeel kitchen composed of individual matching units. He died in Wassenaar, at the age of 92, in September 1977.

3½ ONS 4 ONS 4½ ONS 5 ONS 5½ ONS 6 ONS 6½ ONS

40 GRAM UITSLAG

BIJ DE GROOTSTE WIJZERPLAAT
VAN EEN GEWONE SNELWEGER

40 GRAM UITSLAG

UITSLAG BIJ DE
BERKEL CYCLOPE SCHAAL

Vergelijk nevenstaande uitslagen.
Gevoeligheid 3 × vergroot.
Daardoor contrôle 3 × verscherpt.
Weegmethode en aflezing zeer vereenvoudigd.
Scherpe en duidelijke gradueering. Trillingvrije wijzer.
Speciale lichtreflectie op wijzerkaart.
Duidelijk af te lezen op 5 M. afstand.
Grooter aantal wegingen per tijdseenheid.

HOE GROOTER DUIDELIJKHEID

GEMAKKELIJKER EN

SCHERPER CONTROLE

Page from a brochure designed by Paul Schuitema for Berkel. Reduced.

Paul Schuitema was born in Northern Holland in 1897 in Groningen, which was also Werkman's province. During the period of the first world war he received formal training as a painter, but soon afterwards turned to graphic design. During the early 1920's he became adviser to Berkel, for whom he designed many booklets, folders, and advertisements as well as their trade-mark, stationery, showrooms, and exhibition stands.

From 1926 onwards photography began to play an important role in Schuitema's designs for printed matter. At first he tried to work with professional photographers but found his ideas frustrated by their formal and artistic approach to subjects. By trial and error, however, he soon acquired enough knowledge of photographic technique to achieve the kind of result for which he was searching. He was particularly excited by the effects of motion he found the photograph was able to capture. Some of his photographs and montages were shown at the *Bild und Foto* exhibition in Stuttgart in 1927.

Advertisement for Berkel, 1927.

BERKEL

HET
GROOTSTE
WEEGINSTRUMENTEN
CONCERN TER WERELD

FABRIEKEN TE
ROTTERDAM
TOLEDO - U.S.A.
WINDSOR-CANADA
BRUSSEL
BERLIJN
LONDEN
MILAAN

VOOR

SNELHEID
ECONOMIE
HYGIENE

RESTAURANTS
ZIEKENHUIZEN
GESTICHTEN
HOTELS
CANTINES
SCHEPEN

SNIJDT

WITBROOD
BRUINBROOD
ROGGEBROOD
KOEK
CAKE

SNEL
ECONOMISCH
HYGIENISCH

Advertisements designed by Paul
Schuitema for Berkel c. 1927.

In 1929 he began work on a film, *De Bruggen*. This took as its subject the bridges of
Rotterdam and it was concerned primarily with the movement of things. He followed
it during the 1930's with two other related films: *De Hallen*, which explored the
movement of people, and *De Bouwhoek*, in which it is the camera that moves over an
unmoving landscape.

Schuitema's long career as a teacher began in 1930 when he became a lecturer at the
Royal Academy in The Hague. He continued to teach there until 1963. He died in 1973.

132

Pages from two folders
for Berkel. Reduced.

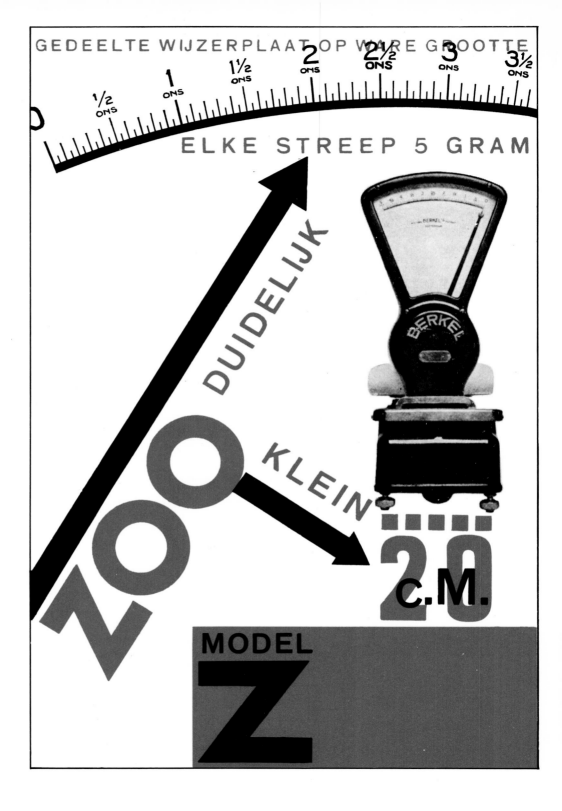

ONZICHTBARE VERLIEZEN ZIJN

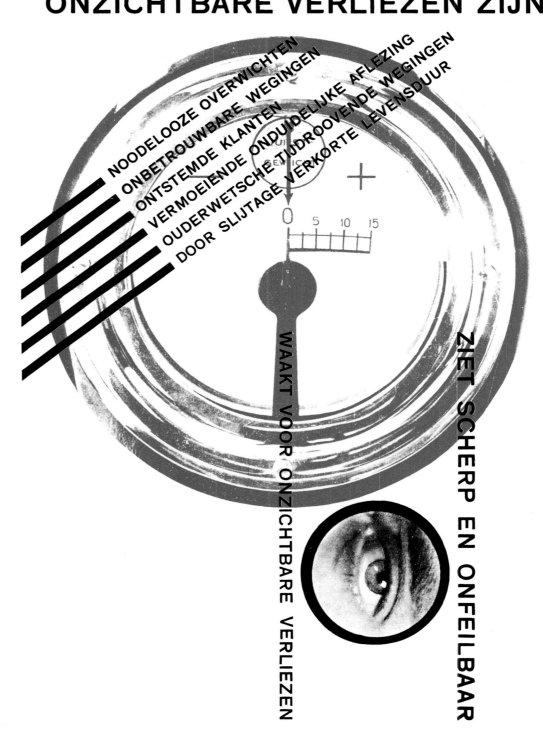

NOODELOOZE OVERWICHTEN

ONBETROUWBARE WEGINGEN

ONTSTEMDE KLANTEN

VERMOEIENDE ONDUIDELIJKE AFLEZING

OUDERWETSCHE TIJDROOVENDE WEGINGEN

DOOR SLIJTAGE VERKORTE LEVENSDUUR

0 5 10 15

WAAKT VOOR ONZICHTBARE VERLIEZEN

ZIET SCHERP EN ONFEILBAAR

Rodchenko's studio stamp.

Cover design by Alexander Rodchenko
for the magazine *Kino-fot*, 1922.

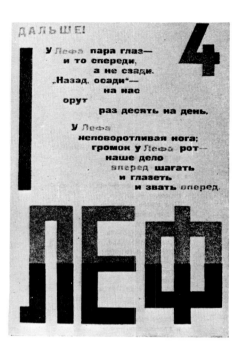

Alexander Rodchenko, 1923. Designs for the cover of *Pro Eto* (About This), and for the covers of two issues of *Lef*.

Alexander Rodchenko was born in St Petersburg in November 1891, but soon after his birth the family moved to Kazan. His father was a stage property maker and until the age of 20, when he enrolled at the local art school, Rodchenko grew up in an entirely theatrical world. At the Kazan school he met Varvara Stepanova whom he later married.

In 1913 Mayakovsky and a group of Futurist poets and painters embarked on a countrywide tour to publicize their ideas. Flamboyantly dressed and with painted faces they read their poetry, showed their paintings, and expounded their views on art to large audiences in hired halls. A visit by this group to Kazan persuaded Rodchenko that he must abandon his course and go to Moscow.

Within a few months of his arrival in Moscow Rodchenko had entirely given up representational painting, and the series of drawings he exhibited, at Tatlin's invitation, in 'The Store' exhibition in Moscow in 1916 were all geometrical compositions produced with compass and ruler in which the circle as a dominant motif is already evident. During the next two years Malevich, who was then nearly 40, as well as Tatlin, exerted considerable influence on Rodchenko as they did also on Lissitzky and many of their other young contemporaries.

By 1920, however, Rodchenko had rejected easel painting and had become one of the most ardent advocates of Constructivism. Under Tatlin, he took over the metalwork department in the Vkhutemas art school and introduced a programme of 'production-art' with the aim of producing 'artist-engineers'. In 1921 he was one of a group of twenty-five artists who announced that they would abandon 'pure art' and devote themselves to industrial design and the applied arts. From this point onwards, Rodchenko concentrated on typographical design.

During 1922 he designed animated film titles for Vertov's documentary newsreels, *Kino-Pravda*, and the following year he took over the layout and typography of the Constructivist magazine *Lef*, collaborated with Mayakovsky on a series of posters – which Mayakovsky called 'the poetry of the street' – and produced cover and page designs for Mayakovsky's poem *Pro Eto*, in which for the first time he employed photomontage. In *Pro Eto* Rodchenko simply used existing published material which he cut out and pasted into his compositions, but later he made his own photographs and he incorporated many of these in his cover designs for *Novi Lef* in 1927 and 1928. In these, and in his photographs for *USSR in Construction* and other magazines during the 1930's, the Constructivist approach with its love of the acutely angled shot is clearly in evidence. During the late 1920's Rodchenko designed more than a dozen Mayakovsky anthologies. At this period he also did much work in the cinema and theatre, and it was then that he first began working as a photo-journalist – an activity which he continued to combine with his work as a typographical designer until his death in Moscow in December 1956.

Slogans on the Mosselprom building in Moscow designed by Rodchenko in collaboration with the poet Mayakovsky.

Cover designs by Alexander Rodchenko
for *Novi Lef*, 1928.

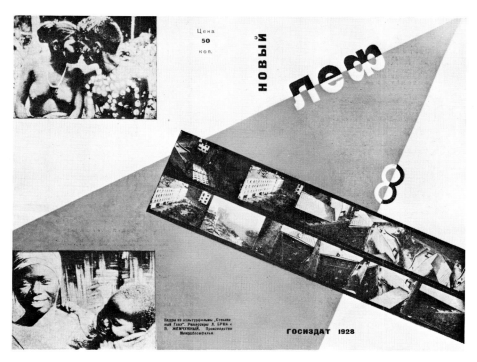

Alexander Rodchenko, 1923.
Photomontage page from
Mayakovsky's *Pro Eto*.

Photograph by Alexander
Rodchenko, 1932.

STAATLICHES BAUHAUS

WEIMAR 1919 1923

BAUHAUSVERLAG G.M.B.H.
MÜNCHEN
MAXIMILIANSTR. 18

Das Buch, welches anläßlich der ersten Ausstellung vom 15. August bis 30. September 1923
des Staatlichen Bauhauses zu Weimar nach
dessen 3½ jährigem Bestehen erscheint, ist in
erster Linie Dokument dieser Anstalt; es reicht
aber, dem Charakter der Anstalt entsprechend,
weit über eine örtliche oder spezifische Ange-
legenheit hinaus ins allgemeine, gegenwärtige
und zukünftige Gebiet künstlerischen Schaffens
und künstlerischer Erziehung.
So wie das Staatliche Bauhaus das erste wirk-
liche Zusammenfassen der im letzten Jahrzehnt
gewonnenen Einsichten in künstlerischen Ent-
wicklungsfragen bedeutet, so nimmt das Buch
spiegelnd Teil an diesen Fragen und bedeutet
jedem, der sich über den Stand dieser Dinge
unterrichten will, hierzu ein willkommenes Mittel.
Darüber hinaus bleibt es ein geschichtliches
Dokument. Denn das Bauhaus ist, obwohl zunächst einzigartig, keine insulare Erscheinung,
sondern ein kräftiger Trieb, der sich voll ent-
faltet und auch völlig sich ausbreiten wird. Das

Bauhaus prospectus designed by Laszlo
Moholy-Nagy, 1923.

Laszlo Moholy-Nagy was born on 20 July 1895 in Borsod in Hungary. At the age of
18 he began to study law in Budapest, but his studies were interrupted by the war and
in 1915 he enlisted in the Hungarian army. He served as an officer in the artillery and in
1917 he was wounded in Russia.

During the war he had produced some drawings, mainly portraits and landscape
subjects, but in 1919, after completing his law studies, he began painting in a non-
representational style that was clearly influenced by the work of Malevich. Before
going to live in Berlin, in 1921, he spent a short period in Vienna. In Germany his
studio became a meeting place for the *avant-garde*, and Lissitzky, van Doesburg, and
Schwitters were frequent visitors. Lissitzky, especially, greatly influenced Moholy-
Nagy's work and ideas at this time. During 1922 Moholy-Nagy had his first exhibition
of paintings, in Berlin, and in September he took part in the meeting of Constructivists
and Dadaists in Weimar.

In March 1923 he was appointed by Walter Gropius to succeed Johannes Itten at the
Bauhaus. This appointment proved to be of the greatest importance to Moholy-Nagy's
personal development and to the evolution of Bauhaus teaching methods and ideas.

Inspired by Man Ray's 'Rayograms' Moholy-Nagy began in 1922 to experiment with
photography and the following year he exhibited and published some of his
photograms. In 1925, his book *Malerei, Photographie, Film* was published as the
eighth volume in the series of Bauhaus books which he edited together with Walter
Gropius. Moholy-Nagy's infectious enthusiasm for photography, his skill and his
ability to verbalize his ideas had great impact on Bauhaus students, and Bauhaus
experiments with photography in the mid 'twenties greatly contributed to the marriage
of photo and type.

In 1928, when Gropius decided to leave the Bauhaus, Moholy-Nagy also resigned.
He returned to Berlin where he designed stage sets for the State Opera and the
Piscator Theatre, made films, and worked as a typographical designer. During 1933
and 1934 he spent some time in Amsterdam and Paris, and in 1935 he moved to
London. In London he again worked with Walter Gropius who had by then
established a partnership with Maxwell Fry, but in 1937 Moholy-Nagy left England to
go to Chicago to found and direct the New Bauhaus, later renamed the Institute of
design. He died in Chicago in 1946.

BAUHAUSBÜCHER

SCHRIFTLEITUNG:
WALTER GROPIUS
L. MOHOLY-NAGY

L. MOHOLY-NAGY:
MALEREI, PHOTOGRAPHIE, FILM

8

L. MOHOLY-NAGY:

MALEREI
PHOTOGRAPHIE
FILM

ALBERT LANGEN VERLAG MÜNCHEN

Title-spread of the eighth volume in the
series of Bauhaus books, published in
1925.

Der Mensch kann im Leben auf vieles nicht achten. Manchmal deswegen, weil seine Organe nicht rasch genug funktionieren, manchmal, weil ihn die Momente der Gefahr etc. zustark in Anspruch nehmen. Auf der Schleifenbahn schließt fast ein jeder die Augen während des großen Stürzens. Der Filmapparat nicht. Im allgemeinen können wir z. B. kleine Babys, wilde Tiere kaum objektiv beobachten, da wir während der Beobachtung eine Reihe von andern Dingen beachten müssen. Im Film ist es anders. Auch eine neue Sicht.

Teufelsrad. Sehr schnell.
Die heruntergeschleuderten Menschen stehen schwankend auf und steigen in einen Zug. Polizeiauto (durchscheinend) rast nach.

In der Bahnhofshalle wird der Apparat erst in **horizontalem** Kreis, dann in **vertikalem** gedreht.
Telegraphendrähte auf den Dächern.
Antennen. Porzellanisolatortürme.
Der TIGER.
Großfabrik.
Rotation eines Rades.
Durchscheinende Rotation eines Artisten.
Salto mortale.
Hochspringen. Hochspringen mit Stab. Fallen. Zehnmal hintereinander.

122

Kasperletheater.
KINDER

UNSER KOPF KANN ES NICHT

10
10 ✕ 10
10

Publikum, wie Wellen des Meeres

Mädchen
Beine.

VaRIETé,
fiebrige Tätigkeit.
Frauenringkampf.
Kitsch.

Jazzbandinstrumente
(Großaufnahme).

Metallkegel- innen leer, glänzend -- wird gegen das Objektiv geschleudert, (inzwischen)
2 Frauen ziehen ihre Köpfe blitzschnell zurück. Großaufnahme.
‹Um das Publikum zu erschrecken. Auch ein dynamisches Moment.›

TEMPO TEMPO
TEMPO

Fußballmatch.
Grob.
Starkes TEMPO.

L. Moholy-Nagy, 1925.
A double-page spread from *Malerei, Photographie, Film.*

An exhibition announcement designed
by Herbert Bayer in 1923.

JULI
AUGUST
SEPT.
1923

BAUHAUS
AUSSTELLUNG WEIMAR

Herbert Bayer, 1925.
Design for a single-alphabet type.

abcdefghi
jklmnopqr
stuvwxyz
a

Herbert Bayer was born at Haag, near Salzburg, in Austria in April 1900. His father was a tax collector in the Salzkammergut and Bayer's early years were spent in this quiet mountainous region. But later the family moved to Linz, and it was to this small provincial town that Bayer returned in 1919, after completing his military service, to become an apprentice to the architect Schmidthammer. A few months later, however, he decided to go to Darmstadt, in Germany, where he worked in the office of Emanuel Margold on a wide variety of commissions ranging from interiors to packaging. In 1921 Bayer enrolled as a student at the Bauhaus in Weimar where he studied first under Kandinsky and, later, under Moholy-Nagy.

In 1923, at the height of the economic crisis in Germany, Bayer was commissioned by the State of Thuringia to design bank-notes in multiples of a million marks. His designs were a complete departure from tradition and made use of a bold sanserif type. They were issued two days later with the ink still wet.

Bayer spent most of 1924 wandering through Italy and Sicily, sketching and painting and sometimes working as a house painter.

A change of government in Thuringia in February 1924 led to the closing of the Weimar Bauhaus, but early in 1925 arrangements were made to transfer the school to Dessau and, in June, Herbert Bayer and five other former students, including Marcel Breuer, Joost Schmidt, and Josef Albers, were appointed teachers. Bayer, who had been put in charge of the typography workshop argued strongly in favour of using a single alphabet, and in 1925 the Bauhaus began to abandon the use of capital letters in its publications. In the same year Bayer produced his first designs for a minimal sanserif type-face in which all the letters were built out of a few selected arcs and straight lines, and only parts which were considered structurally essential were retained.

In February 1928 Gropius, Moholy-Nagy, Breuer, and Bayer left the Bauhaus and Bayer opened a design studio in Berlin. In 1930 he collaborated with Gropius, Breuer, and Moholy-Nagy on the design of the Deutscher Werkbund exhibition in Paris and, in the following year, with Gropius and Moholy-Nagy on the 'Building Workers Unions' exhibition in Berlin.

During his years at Dessau Bayer had been infected by Moholy-Nagy's enthusiasm for

DAS BAUHAUS IN DESSAU

Dessau, Mauerstraße 36   Fernruf 2696   Diskontogesellschaft Filiale Dessau

KATALOG
DER
MUSTER

VERTRIEB

durch die

Cover design by Herbert Bayer for a
catalogue of Bauhaus products, 1925.

147

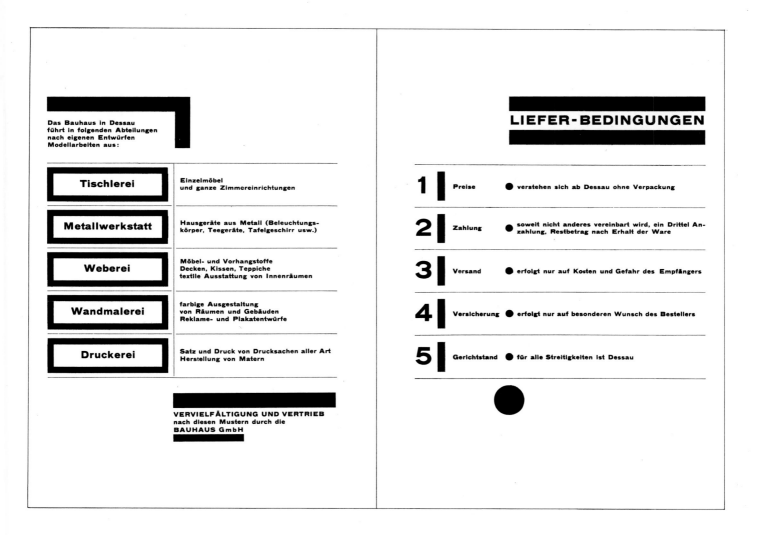

Pages from the catalogue of Bauhaus
products, 1925.

ANHALTISCHER
KUNSTVEREIN
JOHANNISSTR. 13

GEMÄLDE AQUARELLE

KANDINSKY

60.
GEBURTSTAG

Geöffnet:	Wochentags: 2 - 5 nachm.
	Mittwoch u. Sonntag 11 - 1
Eintritt:	Mitglieder: Frei
	Nichtmitglieder: 50 Pfg.

Herbert Bayer, 1926: poster design.

photography as a contemporary means of communication and in Berlin he made extensive use of photo-montage in his advertising and editorial designs. He produced a series of prospectuses for the Berthold typefoundry and cover designs for the magazine *die neue linie*. For Berthold he also designed, in 1933, a geometrically constructed serif typeface called *Bayer-type*. During the 1930's he was for some time art editor of the fashion magazine, *Vogue*.

In 1938 he left Germany for the United States. For many years he lived and worked in Aspen, Colorado. He now lives in California.

Right:
Programme of the Deutsche Werkbund
designed by Herbert Bayer in 1930.

Below:
Herbert Bayer, 1923.
One of a series of bank-notes designed
for the State Bank of Thuringia.

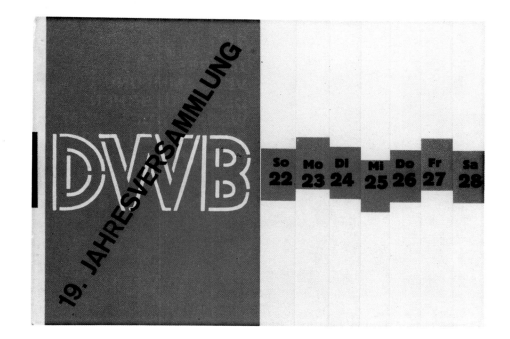

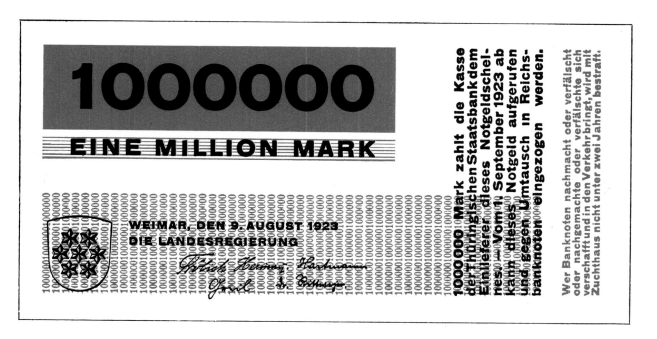

NORMA TALMADGE
IN **KiKi**

**PHOEBUS
PALACE**

SHOWING AT . . . 4ºº 6¹⁵ 8³º
SUNDAYS . . . 1⁴⁵ 4ºº 6¹⁵ 8³º

NACH **CARL STERNHEIM**
MIT WERNER KRAUSS
UND JENNY JUGO

DIE HOSE

**PHOEBUS
PALAST**
ABENDS 4ºº 5¹⁵ 8³º
SONNTAGS 1⁴⁵ 4ºº 6¹⁵ 8³º

ENTWURF: TSCHICHOLD

Two poster designs by Jan Tschichold, 1927.

Jan Tschichold was born in Leipzig in April 1902. Through his father, who was a designer and painter of letters, he developed an early interest in calligraphy. After studying at the Leipzig Academy under Hermann Delitsch he joined the design department of Insel Verlag.

In October 1925 the German printing trade journal *Typographische Mitteilungen* published a special issue, entitled *Elementare Typographie*, written by Tschichold, who was then 23. In this publication Tschichold introduced the typographic work of Lissitzky to a wide audience of practical printers for the first time. Other articles soon followed and during the late 1920's Tschichold ermerged as one of the most ardent and uncompromising advocates of modern typography as well as one of its most skilful exponents. In numerous articles in German and foreign printing trade journals he codified and demonstrated the principles of asymmetrical typography in terms which printers and compositors could readily grasp and could immediately apply in their everyday work. He designed a single-alphabet sanserif type-face, including a phonetic version, and published strong arguments in favour of the use of sanserif types.

In 1926 he was appointed by Paul Renner to teach typography and lettering at the Munich Meisterschule für Deutschlands Buchdrucker and he continued to lecture there until 1933 when, at the Nazis' request, his contract was terminated.

He published his first book *Die Neue Typographie* in 1928, and this was followed two years later by *Eine Stunde Druckgestaltung*. In 1933, when Tschichold was accused by the Nazi Government of 'Kulturbolschevismus' and of creating 'un-German' typography, he left Germany and took refuge in Basle. With the help of Dr Hermann Kienzle, who was then Director of the Basle School of Arts and Crafts, he was offered a teaching appointment and a small retainer by the publishing and printing firm of Benno Schwabe. It was in Switzerland, in 1935, that his next major book, *Typographische Gestaltung*, was published. This book was also published in Danish, Swedish and Dutch and, many years later (in 1967), in English.

Tschichold's work was introduced to England through an exhibition at Lund Humphries in London in November 1935, and this was followed by various assignments including the design of the 1938 volume of *The Penrose Annual*. A well-illustrated article by Tschichold was published by Robert Harling in his magazine

JAN TSCHICHOLD

DIE NEUE TYPOGRAPHIE

EIN HANDBUCH FÜR ZEITGEMÄSS SCHAFFENDE

BERLIN **1928**
VERLAG DES BILDUNGSVERBANDES DER DEUTSCHEN BUCHDRUCKER

Title-page double spread from *Die Neue Typographie*, 1928.

Opposite:
Prospectus for *Die Neue Typographie*, 1928, Reduced. Original in black and yellow.

Typography in the summer of 1937, and in the same year Tschichold visited London to address members of the Double Crown Club on 'A New Approach to Typography'.

Shortly before the beginning of the second world war, Tschichold began gradually to turn away from 'the new typography' – which he then equated with Fascism – and to return to that strictly classical and symmetrical style of typography which he had so fervently, and convincingly, criticised during the preceding decade.

Tschichold continued to live in Switzerland until 1946, when he was engaged by Allen Lane to redesign Penguin books. While working on this commission Tschichold lived in London for three years, but afterwards returned to Switzerland where he lived and worked until his death, at Berzona, near Locarno, in August 1974.

Im VERLAG DES BILDUNGSVERBANDES der Deutschen Buchdrucker,
Berlin SW 61, Dreibundstr. 5, erscheint demnächst:

JAN TSCHICHOLD
Lehrer an der Meisterschule für Deutschlands Buchdrucker in München

DIE NEUE TYPOGRAPHIE

**Handbuch für die gesamte Fachwelt
und die drucksachenverbrauchenden Kreise**

Das Problem der neuen gestaltenden Typographie hat eine lebhafte
Diskussion bei allen Beteiligten hervorgerufen. Wir glauben dem Bedürf-
nis, die aufgeworfenen Fragen ausführlich behandelt zu sehen, zu ent-
sprechen, wenn wir jetzt ein Handbuch der **NEUEN TYPOGRAPHIE**
herausbringen.

Es kam dem Verfasser, einem ihrer bekanntesten Vertreter, in diesem
Buche zunächst darauf an, den engen Zusammenhang der neuen
Typographie mit dem **Gesamtkomplex heutigen Lebens** aufzuzei-
gen und zu beweisen, daß die neue Typographie ein ebenso notwendi-
ger Ausdruck einer neuen Gesinnung ist wie die neue Baukunst und
alles Neue, das mit unserer Zeit anbricht. Diese geschichtliche Notwen-
digkeit der neuen Typographie belegt weiterhin eine kritische Darstel-
lung der **alten Typographie**. Die Entwicklung der **neuen Malerei**, die für alles Neue unserer Zeit geistig bahnbrechend gewesen ist,
wird in einem reich illustrierten Aufsatz des Buches leicht faßlich dar-
gestellt. Ein kurzer Abschnitt „**Zur Geschichte der neuen Typographie**" leitet zu den wichtigsten Teile des Buches, den **Grundbegriffen
der neuen Typographie** über. Diese werden klar herausgeschält,
richtige und falsche Beispiele einander gegenübergestellt. Zwei wei-
tere Artikel behandeln „**Photographie und Typographie**" und
„**Neue Typographie und Normung**".

Der Hauptwert des Buches für den Praktiker besteht in dem zweiten
Teil „**Typographische Hauptformen**" (siehe das nebenstehende
Inhaltsverzeichnis). Es fehlte bisher an einem Werke, das wie dieses Buch
die schon bei einfachen Satzaufgaben auftauchenden gestalterischen
Fragen in gebührender Ausführlichkeit behandelte. Jeder Teilabschnitt
enthält neben **allgemeinen typographischen Regeln** vor allem die
Abbildungen aller in Betracht kommenden **Normblätter** des Deutschen
Normenausschusses, alle andern (z. B. postalischen) **Vorschriften** und
zahlreiche Beispiele, Gegenbeispiele und Schemen.

Für jeden Buchdrucker, insbesondere jeden Akzidenzsetzer, wird „Die
neue Typographie" ein **unentbehrliches Handbuch** sein. Von nicht
geringerer Bedeutung ist es für Reklamefachleute, Gebrauchsgraphiker,
Kaufleute, Photographen, Architekten, Ingenieure und Schriftsteller,
also für alle, die mit dem Buchdruck in Berührung kommen.

typ. tschichold

Das Buch enthält über 125 Abbildungen, von
denen etwa ein Viertel **zweifarbig** gedruckt ist,
und umfaßt gegen **200** Seiten auf gutem Kunst-
druckpapier. Es erscheint im Format DIN A5 (148×
210 mm) und ist biegsam in Ganzleinen gebunden.

Preis bei Vorbestellung bis 1. Juni 1928:   **5.00** RM
durch den Buchhandel nur zum Preise von   **6.50** RM

Bestellschein umstehend ➡

Poster for the Warsaw publisher,
Philobiblon, designed by Jan
Tschichold in 1924. Greatly reduced.
Original in black and gold.

Opposite:
Poster designed by Tschichold, 1937.
Reduced. Original in black and sand-
grey on white paper.

Jan Tschichold, 1929. Design for a
single-alphabet type, above, and for a
phonetic version, below.

für den neuen menschen existiert
nur das gleichgewicht zwischen
natur und geist· zu jedem zeit-

für den noien menſen eksistirt nur
das glaihgeviht tsviſen natur unt
gaist· tsu jedem tsaitpuɾkt der

● vom 16. januar bis 14. februar 1937

kunsthalle basel

konstruktivisten

van doesburg
domela
eggeling
gabo
kandinsky
lissitzky
moholy-nagy
mondrian
pevsner
taeuber
vantongerloo
vordemberge
u. a.

Le Capital
FONDERIE

Transito' a typeface designed by Jan Tschichold for the Amsterdam Type Foundry in 1931.

---

philobiblon eine zeitschrift für bücherliebhaber . a magazine for book-collectors

herbert reichner verlag, wien VI (vienna), strohmayergasse 6

telephon	b 23854
bankkonto	wiener bankverein, wien XIV
postscheckkonten	leipzig 8442
	wien 46469
	prag 501701
	zürich VII 18122

Left:
Letterheading design by Jan Tschichold
for Philobiblon.

Right:
Jan Tschichold: bookjacket, 1931.

Mensch unterm Hammer

Roman von Josef Lenhard

Die sonderbare Geschichte des sonderbaren Proleten
Kilian Narr aus der katholischen bayerischen Pfalz. Un-
bändiger Freiheits- und Wissensdrang bringt ihn unauf-
hörlich in Widerstreit mit allen möglichen Obrigkeiten.
Dieser Kilian Narr ist zur guten Hälfte Josef Lenhard selbst,
der in diesen seinem Erstlingsroman voll bittern Humors
Gericht über sich selbst hält.   In Ganzleinen 4.30 RM

Jan Tschichold:

Typographische Gestaltung

Benno Schwabe & Co . Basel 1935

Title-page for *Typographische Gestaltung*, Basle, 1935. Reduced.

Bojko, Szymon
New Graphic Design in Revolutionary Russia, London 1972

Broos, Kees
Piet Zwart, (Haags Gemeentemuseum) The Hague 1973

Damase, Jacques
Révolution Typographique, Geneva 1966

Elliott, David (Ed.)
Alexander Rodchenko, (Museum of Modern Art) Oxford 1979

Elliott, David (Ed.)
Mayakovsky – Twenty Years of Work, (Museum of Modern Art) Oxford 1982

Gerstner, Karl
The New Graphic Art, Basel 1959

Gray, Camilla
'El Lissitzky, Typographer', *Typographica 16*, London 1959

Gray, Camilla
The Great Experiment: Russian Art 1863–1922, London 1962

Lissitzky-Küppers, Sophie
El Lissitzky – Life, Letters, Texts, London 1968

McLean, Ruari
Jan Tschichold: Typographer, London 1975

Müller, Fridolin (Ed.)
H.N. Werkman, Teufen (Switzerland) 1967

Naylor, G
The Bauhaus, London 1968

Neumann, Eckhard
Functional Graphic Design in the '20s, New York 1967

Schipper, K
Holland Dada, Amsterdam 1974

Wingler, Hans M
The Bauhaus – Weimar, Dessau, Berlin, Chicago, Cambridge, Massachusetts 1969

Paris-Berlin, (Centre Georges Pompidou) Paris 1978

Paris-Moscou, (Centre Georges Pompidou) Paris 1979